5 Marks of Biblical Reformation
by C. Matthew McMahon

Copyright Information

5 Marks of Biblical Reformation by C. Matthew McMahon
Edited by Therese B. McMahon

Copyright ©2019 by Puritan Publications and A Puritan's Mind®

Some language and grammar has been updated from any original manuscripts. Any change in wording or punctuation has not changed the intent or meaning of the original author(s) and has been made to aid the modern reader.

Published by Puritan Publications
A Ministry of A Puritan's Mind® in Crossville, TN.
www.apuritansmind.com
www.puritanpublications.com

This Print Edition, 2019
Electronic Edition, 2019

Manufactured in the United States of America

ISBN: 978-1-62663-339-1
eISBN: 978-1-62663-338-4

Table of Contents

Introduction to Reforming

In our day, the current temperature of the Evangelical church has been watered down by shallow, non-doctrinal preaching that tickles the ears. Their churches are filled with emotionally charged services, catering to jingles that substitute themselves for true worship. People attend churches based on criteria surrounding whether or not the foyer's *coffee shop* serves hot lattes, how short the service is on Sunday so they can get home to mowing the lawn, or whether they can conveniently go to a thirty-minute Saturday night service and disregard the Lord's Day *all-together.* Is this biblical reformation? Not at all. It's quite the opposite.

How many ministers have you met who are sowing reformation in their churches *in tears*? Or for that matter, how many preachers have truly preached in such a way as to set their people on fire through the unction and power of the Spirit of God and his word to reap *something* before God that is spiritually beneficial, heartily *reformed* yet laced with Christian joy? Such considerations should cause us sadness in our own country knowing that in the thousands of churches, maybe millions, across the land, there is not a single united Scriptural *ripple* that is changing the face of the people of God for true Biblical Reformation. Where is the world being turned upside down today as it was in the days of the apostles, or the days of the Reformation, or the days of the Westminster Assembly, or in the days of the preaching of Jonathan Edwards and the revivals of the *Great Awakening?* When have we seen a whole city converted at once as in the days of Calvin, Luther or later during the preaching of Jonathan Edwards? These are sad times to consider such things. Why is it that we have to look back to spiritual giants instead of looking to the right and left of us in the church today?

Christians around the world need true biblical and spiritual reformation. This is what this work is really about: key concepts that are tied to *biblical reform*. Even though God has given Christians blessing upon blessing, mercy piled onto mercy, if we answer God's abundant blessing by sinning against him, what then should we expect? If churches are knee deep in cultural progressivism, and they are merely renewing sins week after week, they are hardly reforming. They are, like Ephraim in Hosea, going in the opposite direction altogether.[1] The hypocritical nature of the Christian church is so apparent, many times, that they are certainly joyful when getting *out of danger or some difficult providence*, but how *little* are they concerned or careful to be *getting out* of *sin, and how much effort are they putting towards being biblically reformed?*[2] Christians *must* be about the work of reformation *post-haste*.

One of the reasons that we don't hear preaching towards biblical reform as it was in the days of old, is

---

[1] "Ephraim, he hath mixed himself among the people," (Hos. 7:8).
[2] "For the congregation of hypocrites shall be desolate," (Job 15:34).

that preachers can't preach well because they don't *think* well;[3] because they are not serious in their study.[4] They need to be taught how to think rightly before they can preach effectively, and they have to study well, before they have something to preach. Seminarians are coming out of seminary thinking they have all they need to step into the pulpit upon graduation; as if 6 credits and 2 homiletics classes will do it. Where will they find the fire of preaching and the unction of the Spirit?[5] They don't even strain to be effective in the pulpit, because they have no real point of reference as to what being effective in the pulpit actually *means*. This, then, translates right down into the pew.

The church today will never see another *Great Awakening* until they get their spiritual act together, and quickly. Do preachers take their office as God's mouthpiece seriously? Do Christians who hear their preachers take it seriously? Certainly, if you ask them, they will tell you *they* think so. It is unfortunate that preachers are just like *American Idol* contestants. Upon audition, they think *they* are best. When they hear some criticism from one of the judges, they have a conniption attack that such a person might even *suggest* such a

---

[3] "Thus saith the LORD, Stand ye in the ways, and see, and ask for the old paths, where is the good way, and walk therein, and ye shall find rest for your souls, " (Jer. 6:16).
[4] "Study to shew thyself approved unto God, a workman that needeth not to be ashamed, rightly dividing the word of truth," (2 Tim. 2:15).
[5] "His word was in mine heart as a burning fire shut up in my bones," (Jer. 20:9).

thing. With preaching, though, there is an affect that must take place. And such an effect is only rewarded by the Spirit, if the preacher is actually preaching the Word and striving for biblical reformation.

Biblical Reformation "back in the day" was a puritan soap box, because it is a *biblical soap box* that *God* started. The reformers and puritans wrote extensively on being reformed by God's word in every area of life. Every Christian ought to jump on that soap box and ride it into eternity. The Christian's duty is manifold, but always comes back to pressing into the kingdom in being reformed by God.[6] The Christian's *duty* should be for godly reform. I have said this many times and in many contexts: it is impossible to document history simply as chronological events, but rather it is the *intrusion* of God into time to establish his *redemptive* purposes in and through men, and declare his person and glory through the work of Jesus Christ.[7] This is the heart of what true biblical reformation is all about. It is being arrested by God in whatever time or culture or place you live in, to be reformed for his glory.[8] Those who cultivate a heart after true biblical Reformation will ultimately see a change in the manner

---

[6] "Since that time the kingdom of God is preached, and every man presseth into it," (Luke 16:16).
[7] "But when the fulness of the time was come, God sent forth his Son, made of a woman, made under the law, to redeem them that were under the law, that we might receive the adoption of sons," (Gal. 4:4-5).
[8] "Whether therefore ye eat, or drink, or whatsoever ye do, do all to the glory of God," (1 Cor. 10:31).

that the Christian religion brings them *coram deo,* before the face of God.[9] Such a Reformation, through the true Gospel of Jesus Christ and justification by faith alone, will unite Christians to God in a more intimate manner than what pop Christianity can offer on some emotional high. Do not be deceived, reader, *pop Christianity* is *not* true biblical Christianity. Evangelicalism does not press for *reformation* any longer. They are more interested in theology dispensed by "Christian cartoons" or popular TV and radio preachers. In general, the term "Evangelical" has developed into a more inclusivistic attitude toward liberalism, and is ecumenical in its worldwide efforts towards "ecclesiastical unity." As a result of a broad churchism this non-theological view is akin to simply pleasing the masses. But it will never bring about reform in Christ's church, if in point of fact, those kinds of churches are even *part* of Christ's body at all!

The Word of God is the only rule for faith and practice in the church where Jesus Christ is Head.[10] This is the only place, only means, where true biblical reformation according to God's prescription can "be done." There is no salvation outside the true church of Christ. Reformation is to be found there. *The 1647*

---

[9] "One thing have I desired of the LORD, that will I seek after; that I may dwell in the house of the LORD all the days of my life, to behold the beauty of the LORD, and to enquire in his temple," (Psa. 27:4).

[10] "And hath put all things under his feet, and gave him to be the head over all things to the church," (Eph. 1:22).

Westminster Confession of Faith says, "But the acceptable way of worshiping the true God is instituted by himself, and so limited by his own revealed will, that he may not be worshiped according to the imaginations and devices of men, or the suggestions of Satan, under any visible representation, or any other way not prescribed in the Holy Scripture." This parallels Calvin's argument throughout his *Necessity of Reforming the Church*. To add or take away from prescribed worship *is sin*. Churches who compromise this principle to uphold some regular aspect of their own fabricated worship compromise the integrity of the Word and their own convictions. Christians, then, who compromise the truth of the Word, become hypocrites; and they may not even know it.[11] Those elders who fail to reform their church by implementing *the Scriptures* upon the life of the congregation compromise the integrity of the Word, and they are, in point of fact, calling God a liar. By not implementing the Word, God is side stepped and man takes center stage. Worship then becomes man-centered rather than Christ-centered. If they truly believed the Word of God, then right worship (corporately and privately) would necessarily be implemented by compulsion to obey God rather than please men. Reformation would occur instead of apostasy and idolatry.

It would be wise for ministers and their flocks to imitate Hezekiah, Josiah, Luther, Calvin and the Lord

---

[11] "Ye blind guides," (Matt. 23:24).

Jesus Christ in the achievement of immediate reformation.[12] Compromise is a lie. True Biblical Reformation for both the church and the Christian is biblically *necessary*.

To help us all along on our Christian journey toward godly reform, I have outlined five marks of biblical reformation. Mark 1: Spiritual Growth, Mark 2: Guarding the Heart, Mark 3: The Sin of Partial Reformation, Mark 4: How Reformation and Prayer are Linked Together, and Mark 5: The Spirit of God in Biblical Reformation. They are all applicable both individually to the believer and corporately to the church at large. Without understanding these simple and biblical ideas, reformation in the church will never get off the ground.

In addition to taking all this in and considering it, pray that true biblical reformation would affect every sphere that Christians are engaged in. The church, the home, the workplace, the state, the country your live in, in fact, all of society throughout the world for the glory of the great King, Jesus Christ, and the Kingdom of God. May it be said, as it was of the apostles when they strove for biblical reform under the Spirit's leading and power, "These that have turned the world upside down are come hither also," (Acts 17:6).

---

12 "And his disciples remembered that it was written, the zeal of thine house hath eaten me up," (John 2:17).

Mark 1: Spiritual Growth in Biblical Reformation

"Wherefore laying aside all malice, and all guile, and hypocrisies, and envies, and all evil speakings, as newborn babes, desire the sincere milk of the word, that ye may grow thereby: if so be ye have tasted that the Lord is gracious," (1 Peter 2:1-3).

We find here in 1 Peter the apostle's general epistle to the church at large. Peter writes to the churches with a message of hope, and with a message of practicality. It ends with a great deal of doctrinal importance, not to say that the first couple of chapters have no doctrine: for all Scripture is useful, and all Scripture holds in it solid biblical doctrine. It is foolish to call one's self a Christian because one simply knows things about God. Demons believe truth as well, but we would never call them *Christians*. Rather, Peter's starting point in the first two chapters presses the reader to listen to practical reasons for holiness.

The elect are saved through the grace of the Father, the knowledge of Christ, and sanctified by the Spirit, "unto obedience." Such obedience is covered in Christ's holy blood, where they are sprinkled, by the blood of the new covenant by the new Testator.[1] In this God is seen by Peter, and should be by the reader, as *blessed forever.*

Not only is God forever to be praised because of who he is, but because also of what he has done through Christ.[2] They receive an inheritance that can never be shaken or fade. They are kept by God's power, grounded in faith. In all this there is rejoicing for God's priceless provision of salvation.

While this knowledge of God is cause for rejoicing, still, these Christians Peter writes to are being persecuted. Faith that is tried is precious in God's sight because it renders the Christian more conformed to Jesus Christ, and God loves to see Christ's image formed in Christians; that is the hallmark of holiness.[3] And these readers are exhorted that though they have not seen Christ with their eyes, they still love him. Such belief is a cause for joy and establishes their faith in all trials and temptations.

He then presses them to consider the work of the Spirit on their mind, that they may be able to endure these difficult times. To press forward in holiness, *for* God is holy. And he does not quote the traditions of the fathers or the law merely to set his context, but to show

---

[1] "For where a testament is, there must also of necessity be the death of the testator," (Heb. 9:16).

[2] "I will praise thee for ever, because thou hast done it: and I will wait on thy name; for it is good before thy saints," (Psa. 52:9).

[3] "For whom he did foreknow, he also did predestinate to be conformed to the image of his Son," (Rom. 8:29).

them that they need to live in holiness and the fear of God because they have not been bought with the blood of bulls and goats, but with the precious blood of Christ. Foreordained before the foundation of the world in the Covenant of Redemption to save his people from their sins. He died, was raised from the dead, and is believed on by faithful, holy Christians, as Peter says, *like you.* These are those who obey the truth by the power of the Spirit. Such truth was preached to them, and they believed it to the saving of their souls.

"Therefore," as a result of all this, I have some directives for you, Peter is saying. As a result of God's eternal and everlasting covenant,[4] Christ's redemptive work, the Spirit's motions to your holiness, your belief in the preached word, and even amidst all these trials, there are certain duties you must adhere to. This is no legalism. This is obedience. There is a great difference between legalism and obedience. The former is often used as negative slang to dismiss the latter. "Laying aside all malice, all deceit, hypocrisy, envy, and all evil speaking." The phrase "laying aside" is akin to Zech. 3:3 and the need for Joshua the High Priest to be clothed with new garments.[5] Laying aside that which is filthy is not so easily done. Ephesians speaks of laying aside lying (4:25). Colossians speaks of laying aside evil practices

---

[4] "Incline your ear, and come unto me: hear, and your soul shall live; and I will make an everlasting covenant with you, even the sure mercies of David," (Isa. 55:3).
[5] "Now Joshua was clothed with filthy garments, and stood before the angel," (Zech. 3:3).

(3:9). Hebrews speaks of laying aside weights that weigh down (12:1), besetting sins. Take off the old man and put on the new man. Take off the old garments and put on new garments. Garments sprinkled by blood, covered in the blood of Christ. "But put on the Lord Jesus Christ, and make no provision for the flesh, to fulfill its lusts," (Rom. 13:14). However, sin is not something that Christians can simply brush away, or simply lay aside like a cloak. How wonderful would it be to easily wash remaining sin off with a bar of soap?

Peter may be better understood by seeing what he is saying in this way, "Abandon doing any kind of sin." God is holy. Be holy like he is; without which no one will see the Lord.[6] Thanks be to Christ who makes Christians holy through the Spirit!

These sins mentioned, malice, deceit, *etc.*, are all offences against everything that requires the Christian to be holy like God, yet, are in special relationship to act in opposition to the "love of the brethren" which was part of the substance of chapter 1. It is not a list of things for individual, hidden sins, but specifically in relation to one another as a body. Being holy together; being holy as part of Christ's mystical body. Those old cloaks must all be discarded if one is truly sprinkled by the blood of Christ in their conscience and has a love of the brethren.

Then he gives them a positive, practical direction with an argument, together, with a qualifier, "as newborn babes, desire the pure milk of the word, that

---

[6] "...for the LORD our God is holy," (Psa. 99:9).

you may grow thereby." The practical direction is as newborn babes to desire the pure milk of the word. *Newborn babes* in this context are those born of incorruptible seed, begotten by the death and resurrecting power of God's Anointed Savior and Redeemer. Peter may have been thinking about the words of Christ here, "Unless you are converted and become as little children, you will by no means enter the kingdom of heaven," (Matt. 18:3). Little children, by way of their physical necessity, are dependent on others for a great portion of their life. They are unable to fend for themselves, really in any way, until they grow up. Newborn babes, the designation of all those born into Christ's kingdom, are always *dependent* in this way. Some think that this verse may be such that Peter is speaking of recent coverts to whom he is writing. I find this, though, a stretch on the text. Entering the kingdom of God happens on conversion, but also happens upon glorification. Unless you become like little children...you will not enter, in either sense. I think this is bigger than simply conversion. Desire means to long for it eagerly (ἐπιποθήσατε), as babes long for milk. Their food is milk. This is appropriate and suitable to them at that age. It is for babies, the only food necessary for them. Such a desire for proper food will be for the Christian who desires the word. The word is their only proper food. At what point do they grow out of this? The pure milk of the word is longed for. The word of God for newborns, or those growing, or those in adulthood, is the proper food for Christians. It is the means of grace by which the eternal covenant of the sprinkled blood of Christ is ministered to the saint.

The argument from this desire of pure milk is that such will grow by this. In some of the more ancient biblical Greek translations the word "salvation" is found there, "that by it you may grow in respect to salvation" (1 Peter 2:2). In either case the meaning is still the same and does not change Peter's intent. Under the sprinkling of the blood of Christ, in his eternal covenant to save his people, those who believe by faith are to be like newborn babes desiring that which will tend to their support, their provision and their strengthening, their food.[7] They grow in grace and salvation only through the practical working of the word of God in all its means of grace. This is only found in and among those in the church.

"If indeed you have tasted that the Lord is gracious." This is the practical qualifier. Newborn babes continue to drink pure milk when the milk is good for them. They will not drink spoiled milk. Christians, in this same light, are to drink of the pure, unspoiled milk of the word, but, they do so if they have tasted that the Lord is gracious. Tasting was done upon conversion, and as a result of having this taste, if that has happened to them as newborns, so they should desire this, long for it, and eagerly drink of it, always. Peter is quoting Psalm

---

[7] See even Christ's explanation of those converts coming into the kingdom by being "born" from above in John 3.

34:8, "Oh taste and see that the Lord is good!" This applies to how the Lord is good through the sprinkling of Christ's blood, and their being birthed of incorruptible seed. Those who taste in this way are blessed by God.

The phrase "the Lord is gracious" really is better translated as the "Lord is good." The word can be extrapolated to mean *gracious*, because when God is good to his people he is being gracious to them, but the idea is really the meaning of the psalmist, and the main translation of the word "kindness or goodness" in Greek. God is good. Christ is good. Taste the goodness of the Lord. But both the Psalmist and Peter are pressing the reader to consider and discover the goodness of God by experience.

Consider this doctrine coming from Peter's text, that the pursuit of holiness and spiritual growth in Christ's church is accomplished experimentally through the Word of God, and this is the only means of spiritual reformation. There is no biblical reformation without this pursuit of holiness, for such is the pursuit of the Scriptures and the will of God for life and godliness.[8] Growing in this way presupposes the pursuit of holiness. If a person is going to uphold God's Law, and continue in conformity to it, they will in fact glorify God in upholding and imitating the character of God. The only place Christians find the path of life and godliness

---

[8] "...but godliness is profitable unto all things, having promise of the life that now is, and of that which is to come," (1 Tim. 4:8).

is in the Scriptures. It is true, God's invisible attributes and divine power are found in the practical working of creation. But the specific rule of faith, the entire embodiment of holiness, is found in the special revelation of God's divine word. Hold that thought for a moment.

There must be a pursuit of holiness in the church. Have you ever considered that holiness is to be church-wide? There is the pursuit of holiness in the church, "to Him be glory *in the church,"* (Eph. 3:21). "God has appointed these *in the church:* first apostles, second prophets, third teachers, after that miracles, then gifts of healings, helps, administrations, varieties of tongues," (1 Cor. 12:28). All these are for the edification of the mystical body. "Now you are the body of Christ, and members individually," (1 Cor. 12:27). "But as He who called you is holy, you also be holy in all your conduct," (1 Peter 1:15). This is done and mimicked by the church because God is holy. The church is a "chosen generation, a royal priesthood, a holy nation, His own special people, *[why?]* that you may proclaim the praises of Him who called you out of darkness into His marvelous light," (1 Peter 2:9). Light is truth.[9] It is the church's banner and standard to proclaim the light. They are to proclaim the

---

[9] "But if we walk in the light, as he is in the light, we have fellowship one with another, and the blood of Jesus Christ his Son cleanseth us from all sin," (1 John 1:7). "But is now made manifest by the appearing of our Saviour Jesus Christ, who hath abolished death, and hath brought life and immortality to light through the gospel," (2 Tim. 1:10).

truth, which is the character of God pressed into the Christian made possible because of the work of Christ on the soul.

For the church to continue in the pursuit of holiness this must be pursued in little churches – Christian homes. Simeon Ashe said, "The house of the godly is a little church; just as the house of the wicked a little hell."[10] Even in homes the pursuit of holiness is to be a small reflection of the growth found in the body of the church. If individuals are not growing, the church will not collectively grow. Here we find the basics of devotional and family life. But without holiness in the individual, without holiness at home, there will be no furthering of holiness in the church.

The pursuit of holiness for the church is set in the context of being newborn babes. Newborn babes are not taught to eat. They know how to do that even as they emerge from the womb. They drink milk, they cry about wanting more, and such is programmed into their nature by God for their physical growth. Must Christians be taught to spiritually eat? In many ways, yes. This is why, for example, James says, "let every man be swift to hear," (James 1:19). Hearing and consequently experiencing the word in all its forms is the meat and drink of the means of grace. This is something to be done by all professing Christians in the church. That they may grow up into the stature of Christ together. They are all members of

---

[10] Ashe, Simeon, *A Treatise on Divine Contentment*, (Coconut Creek, FL: Puritan Publications, 2012) 119.

one mystical body, but they are growing together in one local body.[11]

The pursuit of holiness has a dimension to it that is done together. It is true that individuals must pursue holiness. But this is never done in a vacuum. It is done in the midst of the body of Christ. There are no *Lone Ranger* Christians. God has not setup obedience, the pursuit of holiness, spiritual growth, for each member to achieve individually on their own.[12] If this were the case there would be no need of preaching. There would be no need of spiritual gifts. There would be no need for Paul to say that all Christians are part of one body.[13] There would be no need for the Psalmist to say how wonderful it is when he congregates together with the saints. There would be no preference for God to prefer to be in the midst of the congregation of his collected saints in Zion over the individual tents of Jacob. There would be, then, no mystical body of Christ, really. Christianity is a religion of mutual fellowship and growth. Holiness, spiritual growth in God, is often utilized through and by one another. Encourage one another while it is still called today.[14] Even families are *families*, not lone individuals.

---

[11] "There is one body, and one Spirit, " (Eph. 4:4).
[12] "For we being many are one bread, and one body: for we are all partakers of that one bread," (1 Cor. 10:17).
[13] Rom. 12:4-5; 1 Cor. 6:16, 10:17, 12:12-13, 20; Eph. 2:16, 4:4; Col. 3:15.
[14] "But exhort one another daily, while it is called To day; lest any of you be hardened through the deceitfulness of sin," (Heb. 3:13).

It is an absurd notion in the manner in which God has set up the human condition in his providence, to allow people to remain autonomous from others. "Religion is personal for me" you hear people say. Or, "I don't like organized religion, but I love God." No, no they don't. This is merely a cloak for their sin. How can one love Jesus and not love his church?[15] They don't want other people telling them what to do, or how to behave and such. Collective family religion is found as one the most powerful instruments for the spiritual growth of the church. If the family suffers in the pursuit of holiness and spiritual growth, the church suffers. All these intricate parts working together. All these parts are doing their job as members of the body. All these parts are working toward a single goal as the singular bride of Christ.[16]

The pursuit of holiness and biblical reformation in this way is confirmed by experience. The church needs to know what the Word is. The light of nature and the works of creation and providence, manifest the goodness, wisdom, and power of God. Such works cause men to be without excuse in rendering and submitting to the holiness of God. However, such works of creation and providence are not sufficient to give the saving knowledge of God, and the saving nature of his will. The Holy Scriptures are necessary to reveal God's holy

---

[15] "...even as Christ also loved the church, and gave himself for it," (Eph. 5:25).
[16] "Come hither, I will shew thee the bride, the Lamb's wife," (Rev. 21:9).

prescription for life. Christians pray, "Your will be done..."[17] They think that if they tack on to their prayers this little phrase that makes their prayers OK. "See, now I've prayed according to God's will," they think. No, God's will is revealed in Scripture, and it is up to the Christian and the church to pray, walk, talk, live and die according to what the *Scriptures say.* They must rightly apply the Scriptures to them for everything needed in life and godliness in the pursuit of holiness; and in the pursuit of biblical reform. They ought, then to be desiring the pure milk of the word.

From the canon of Scripture, from Genesis to Revelation, as set down by God, these Scriptural books were given by inspiration of God.[18] They are the rule of faith and practice, not just faith. Spiritual growth, especially in these times of the Gospel, and the fulfillment of the *Covenant of Redemption* by Jesus Christ, is the only means by which the Spirit works to further cleanse the bride of Christ from sin.[19] Every means of grace is a fashioning of the Scriptures to the life of the believer by the power of the Spirit. Only in the Word, the Living Word, are Christians sanctified in their pursuit of holiness. God's Word permeates every aspect of the church: church life, fellowship, the means

---

[17] Matthew 6:10.

[18] "All scripture is given by inspiration of God, and is profitable for doctrine, for reproof, for correction, for instruction in righteousness," (2 Tim. 3:16).

[19] Luke 22:29; Heb. 7:22; Gal. 3:17; Psalm 119:122; Isa. 38:14; Zech. 6:13.

of grace, family and private devotions; all of those are regulated and governed by the church, the Word *preached*. The Word *visibly participated in* – the Supper. The Word sung in the Psalms. The Word *prayed*. The Word *studied*. The Word *meditated* on. The Word *shared;* the Word given *testimony;* the Word *exercised* in practical godliness. *Jesus is the Word,* (John 1:1). It is more of Jesus in every form. Once such Christians wrap their minds around the Word ministered to them in all these ways, once they taste of it, once they experience it, they desire it more. This is why the Psalmist tells the Christian in Psalm 1 that it is on the word that one meditates day and night,[20] and if such is accomplished according to God's rules, he will be like a tree planted by rivers of water. It flourishes with fruitfulness. The Word should be, then *everything* to the Christian. They should live well by the book and die for the book if necessary. In doing so they live and die for the Word, which is Christ; if God so wills.

Theology is doctrine or teaching of living to God through Christ by the Word.[21] William Ames, marries the truth of the definition to its practical application when he says, "Theology is doctrine or teaching of living

---

[20] "But his delight is in the law of the LORD; and in his law doth he meditate day and night," (Psa. 1:2).

[21] Peter van Mastricht, *Theoretico-Practica Theologia*, I.i.16 quoted in Mueller, Richard, *Post Reformation Reformed Dogmatics*, Volume 1, (Grand Rapids, Baker Academic: 2003) 156. See also, van Mastricht, Peter, *Theoretical Practical Theology*, Volume 1: Prolegomena (The Dutch Reformed Translation Society, Grand Rapids, MI: Reformation Heritage Books, 2018) 113.

to God." William Perkins stated that "Theology is the science of living blessedly forever."[22] It is confirmed by experience and the testimony of the Spirit in the heart of the believer. The Christian can read in Scripture that they should pray. They know they should. They hear all arguments for it. They want to. But if they do not *do it*, the experience they should gain from it will never occur. This is true of every manifestation of the Word in their life. Praying, reading, studying, meditating and the like. *To taste* something does not mean then *know it*.

Consider this and reflect on it: the sopadilla packs a sugary punch with its extremely sweet, sunset-colored interior. It has the flavor of a caramelized pear, which means it can basically be dessert. Knowing that a sopadilla tastes like a sopadilla is not knowing what a sapodilla tastes like. Knowing what godly mediation is, is not experiencing the fruit of it by experience. In his wisdom, God made the pursuit of holiness and the spiritual advancement of the Christian by experience, and yet, not by osmosis. One must be a doer of the word not only a hearer of the word. One must not be one who is zapped in some way or thinks that biblical reform comes merely by being zapped by the Spirit. This is never the case.

There are five hindrances to spiritual growth in the pursuit of holiness and biblical reformation. Hindrance 1: being a carnal man under the power of

---

[22] McMahon, Matthew C., The *Reformed Apprentice Volume 4: Private Devotions*, (Crossville, TN: Puritan Publications, 2017).

Satan. Such men do not long for the pure milk of the word. They long for the spoiling delicacies of the world. It is a great disadvantage for a man to be without a weapon in the midst of his enemies, even captured by them. Carnal security comes from both traditions and sinful habits. They never rely on God's protection in the word, but work from an unconverted heart, who have a form of godliness but deny its power. They rely on outward means, or on their own strength and wisdom. In this they turn away from God...cursed is the one who trusts in man. They are not secured from evil but secured under its power. They remain under the prince of this world, and he rules them with chains and servitude to sin. No carnal man ever grew one inch in the sight of God. They are spiraling down in the opposite direction heating hell hotter in the aggravation of their sin. One must be born again in order for them to see spiritual truth (John 3:3-10).

Hindrance 2: not being familiar with the Word. This is the plight of most Christians because they have not learned how to study. In the book of Ezekiel there is spiritual nourishment for the Christian, the pure milk of the word, and if it is not read or studied, the Christian cannot be familiar with that Word for Gospel growth. Christ is the charioteer in Ezekiel 1. He is the one who sits on God's chariot throne. He is the one who commands the chariot and the wheels in Ezekiel 10. He is the one whose right it is to rule the church in Ezekiel 21:27. He is the True Shepherd in Ezekiel 34. It ends by saying "the Lord is there." God *with us*. Ezekiel fuels the book of Revelation to a great extent. Ezekiel is *full* of Christ. The fuel of public or private worship is knowledge of the word. The more the Christian knows, the more he is able to draw closer to God. The Christian cannot grow without successive knowledge being built up.[23] To know one thing is to know it. To know two things, is to know more. To know Genesis is to know one book. To know the Old Testament is to know 39 books. Where knowledge of the Word grows, the Christian grows. But knowledge must give way to wisdom. It must not only be familiar, but it must practically motion the Christian towards holiness.

Biblical reformation must include both knowledge and practice. How can one discern God's will in the Word, unless they have knowledge, and rightly apply that knowledge? How can a person discern that knowledge is good without practice? Theory will never get one out of the library into the laboratory. What is discernment? How do knowledge and discernment intertwine? Discernment is the peculiar gift of those who exercise wisdom with knowledge. Wisdom is the right application of knowledge and a hearty discernment is the result of the careful scrutiny of knowledge applied with a wise biblical mind. But this can only happen as Christians are filled with knowledge – knowledge of the Word, applied. One can never have

---

[23] "But grow in grace, and in the knowledge of our Lord and Saviour Jesus Christ," (2 Peter 3:18).

wisdom without knowledge. How then can one be *wise unto salvation* without knowing what that means and how that practically works out in life? It is the same as saying, *be wise unto holiness.*

Christians must be exhorted to get a knowledge of the word and hold onto it. Prov. 2:1 says, "My son, if thou wilt receive my words, and hide my commandment within thee," then verse 5, "then shalt thou understand the fear of the Lord, and find the knowledge of God." Familiarity with the word cultivates knowledge of God. "Let the word of God dwell in you richly in all wisdom, teaching and admonishing one another," (Col. 3:16). As the Word dwells in the Christians, so God dwells in the Christian. Christ *is* the word. Christians should ever have God's word in their hearts and mouths. Being unfamiliar with the word is like being unfamiliar or without a weapon in the midst of battle. Christian maturity is not constituted by age, but by depth of knowledge of the Word of God and therefore of God himself. Only this can bring a proper fear of God to your heart, and a true biblical reformation to your life.

Imagine all the older people (all those gray heads) in so many churches all over the world who have little knowledge of God though they have attended their church for *decades.* They attend thinking that further attendance, commitment to the pew they sit in, will in some way earn them a more sanctified life. They know little to nothing and can offer no real Scriptural support for their faith or the command to encourage one another using Scriptural principles. Hebrews warns, "For though by this time you ought to be teachers, you need someone to teach you again the first principles of the oracles of God," (Heb. 5:12).

Hindrance 3: after hearing the word, not doing what the Word says will hinder biblical reformation. Spiritual growth built on sound doctrine, with a practical life application of those doctrines, is a sure sign of a growing congregation under Christ. What they believe will determine how they live. But this is only something that happens when they hear what the word says and do what the word says. Put off sin, put on holiness. This is Peter's exhortation: *put off sin, put on holiness.* Do this as a church. The Word of God, which is able to save souls and is used by the Holy Spirit in all ordinary instances of conversion, has three important facets outside of being inspired, inerrant and infallible. The Scriptures are complete (stressing unification of all its parts), clear (stressing that even the most unlearned can read them and be knowledgeable concerning the way of salvation) and sufficient (stressing that there is no need for anything other than the Scriptures to determine the substance of faith and practice for the Christian). Doers of the Word are blessed in their deeds, where mere professors are self-deceivers, who satisfy themselves with a faith that does not work and is dead. *Christians observe in order to do.* Hearing and not doing is called in Scripture *hypocrisy and sin.* They delude themselves if they only hear and leave off doing what the

Word says. This, however, implies that they have a knowledge, at least of what the word says. They cannot plead ignorance. They only plead non-conformity to what God says.

Hindrance 4: unrepentant sin hinders biblical growth and reformation. Sin *hinders* spiritual growth. Andrew Gray said, "Sin is the adulteress that lies between you and your husband. O, the bitterness of sin, that keeps you from the sweet feast of God."[24] Sin hinders every aspect of Christian sanctification. Sin hinders closing with Christ at conversion. Sin hinders seeing Christ clearly as a Christian. Sin, by degrees, and not often all at once, will erode working grace. The Christian deals with a principle that cannot be taken away but can be made of less practical effect. The cherishing of sin is the withering of grace. Besetting sins, or having an eye on any one special sin, hinders the growth of grace.[25] It makes grace in the Christian more undiscernible. When those sins are entertained, the active working of grace in spiritual growth and the pursuit of holiness ceases. It reverses. This is the road backsliders take into apostasy. If a Christian lives habitually in sin, this acts like a destructive worm at the root of the plant. Grace cannot thrive there.

---

[24] Gray, Andrew, *A Door Opening into Everlasting Life*, (Coconut Creek, FL: Puritan Publications, 2013) 270.
[25] "Let us lay aside every weight, and the sin which doth so easily beset us, and let us run with patience the race that is set before us," (Heb. 12:1).

In our yard, in some soil, certain plants will not grow. If one of the plants in our garden withers and shrivels and looks as if it is dying, I look at the ground, at the root, and I find worms gnawing the root; and this is the cause of the plant slowly dying. Sin is like this. It hinders communion with God because it hinders vital communication with God; which in turn promotes holiness through the word. It grieves the Spirit, and the Spirit is the means by which Christians are illuminated. When illumination dissipates, there is no growth in the Word. Sin causes Christians to have a great hinderance in enjoying that close fellowship.

Hindrance 5: not seeking the illumination of the Spirit for biblical reformation. There is a special work of the Spirit of God on the minds of Christians. The Spirit communicates spiritual wisdom, light, and understanding to them through the Bible. This is important both in personal study and in the midst of the congregation in teaching and preaching. This is a very necessary tool so that they might know and practically apply the mind of God to their Christian walk. They will never understand holiness, the divine instruction of spiritual growth, or any of the mysteries of godliness without the illuminating work of the Spirit. The Christian life is useless without the motioning of the Spirit and empowering by him.[26] Christians must seek the Spirit for this work in connection with spiritual growth and the pursuit of holiness. John Owen said,

---

[26] "If we live in the Spirit, let us also walk in the Spirit," (Gal. 5:25).

"That there is a special work of the Holy Spirit, in the supernatural illumination of our minds, needful to the end proposed, — namely, that we may aright, and according to our duty, understand the mind of God in the Scripture ourselves, or interpret it to others."[27] "Open my eyes, that I may see wondrous things from Your law," (Psa. 119:18).

The psalmist asks for help. John records, "These things I have written to you who believe in the name of the Son of God, that you may know that you have eternal life, and that you may continue to believe in the name of the Son of God," (1 John 5:13). *Know*, plus the practical working of *believing*. This is biblical reform in knowledge and practice.

The communication of such a supernatural and divine light from God is the particular work of the Holy Spirit. He is the author of all spiritual illumination. He shines the light of the Gospel of Christ on all the pages of Scripture. Only through the power of the Spirit is a Christian able to know or understand the mind of God in the Scripture in the way God requires. The Christian then, must always pray for the illumination of the Spirit in this so that they may understand the word, and that it may be rightly applied. Gospel growth or the pursuit of holiness in this way for biblical reformation in the church is of necessity. Christians who do not have spiritual growth have spiritual decay. We call this

---

[27] Owen, John. *The Works of John Owen*, Volume 4 (Carlisle, PA: The Banner of Truth Trust, 1994) 126.

spiritual declension (moral deterioration). If the believer would reach Peter's exhorted establishment in spiritual comfort, he must strive to daily grow in grace. It must be his earnest and continual endeavor, in the faith of God's free favor to him, to grow stronger and stronger in all those duties God requires of him, preparing him for work among the body of believers. He is to abound more and more in the exercise of every grace implanted by the Holy Spirit in his soul. If he does this, spiritual declension (and even the loss of spiritual comfort) will be prevented. Otherwise, their foot shall slip in due time.[28] The apostle Peter, in order to prevent the believers to whom he wrote, from being so led away with the error of the wicked, as to fall from their own steadfastness directed them to "grow in grace." It is their collective duty, as well as of privilege, to "increase with the increase of God", to "grow up into Christ who is the head," not only in all things, but at all times. They ought at all times, to grow inwardly, by faith and love, holding onto more firmly Christ, the fountain of grace and all spiritual influences. They are to grow by being more and more holy, and more and more fruitful in good works of righteousness. To grow in grace is to grow continually in it until the day one is translated to the celestial city. There is only growth verses death, only biblical reformation, or spiritual deterioration. There is no

---

[28] "...their foot shall slide in due time: for the day of their calamity is at hand, and the things that shall come upon them make haste," (Deut. 32:35).

neutrality. It is advancing verses retreating. It is walking alone verses walking together towards being sanctified towards holiness. And all of this occurs through the illuminating power of the Spirit by the Word of life.

It is not enough to read the word, nor enough to hear the word preached, nor enough to listen to a lesson taught. You must *experience* the Word. This is far different than having a form of godliness but denying its power (2 Tim. 3:5). How do you experience the Word? *Do you* experience it? If someone were to ask you, how did you experience God in the Word in the past week for your good and growth, what would you say? It should never be, "I don't know." It is never enough to thread the word of God through your eyes as you read it, but that you must *taste* it. It is never enough to hear the word preached, for example, you must taste the word preached, for there is such a thing as spiritually tasting the word. Thomas Manton said, "To a spiritual taste the word of God is sweeter than all pleasures and delights whatsoever."[29] The soul has its senses as well as the body. The Spirit of God leaves an impression on the soul, through the mind. "Moreover He said to me, "Son of man, eat what you find; eat this scroll, and go, speak to the house of Israel." So I opened my mouth, and He caused me to eat that scroll. And He said to me, "Son of man, feed your belly, and fill your stomach with this scroll that I give you." So I ate, and it was in my mouth like

---

[29] Manton, Thomas, *The Complete Works of Thomas Manton*, Volume 8, (Worthington, IL: Maranatha Publications, 1979) 43.

honey in sweetness," (Ezek. 3:1-3). No, God did not tell him to read the scroll, not merely read the Word, or listen to God read it to him, the prophet must *eat it and digest it.*

Do you see yourself as a newborn babe? In the sense that you are wholly reliant like a babe desiring the pure milk of the Word? Always? You might say, "when do we outgrow this?" The answer is, in this life, never, but only into the life to come. Why ought you to desire these things? "That you may grow thereby, if indeed you have tasted that the Lord is gracious," (1 Peter 2:2-3). God requires you to prove out your conversion. Doesn't he know you are converted? Yes. But...be like little children who have tasted something good to eat and desire more. Of course, this is only possible if you have found that God is good to you by knowledge and *experience.* Give a child a piece of candy and do they rest content? I think not. They will eat it until they are sick or stopped. You ought to eat to be filled, and this constantly. You must not be content to take another's word for it. Such tasting occurred at your conversion from the forgiveness of your sins. Are you done with that? Is there no more forgiveness to be had? It is true that Christ's imputed righteousness covers you completely as one converted. One cannot be declared more just than they are right now by God on account of Jesus Christ. But justification is not the same as sanctification. There is more sanctification to be had in your mortal bodies in practical living.[30] We are not speaking about simply being justified and converted. We are speaking about practically being conformed to Christ's image. Keeping it overly simple, justification gets you into the kingdom, and sanctification makes you more like the King. If you are saved, you have the first, but are always in need of more of the second. How do you get this – this holiness and sanctification, this biblical reformation of life? Through the Spirit and your devotion to the word in all its forms. You must diligently and highly esteem the Word of God. When you do, you highly esteem the Lord Jesus Christ, the Eternal Word – the Logos of God. Remember, the Father is seeking worshippers (John 4:23-24). Is it not interesting that Jesus does not say that God is seeking saved individuals?[31] He is seeking *worshippers*. He seeks them by the Spirit, sent of the Messiah, the Christ, through the Word of God, who is the GREAT GOD. Christ, as he so says in the first chapter of John, is not only the Word of God, but is the perfect exegete of the Father. Christ is the fullness of the Godhead, and is expressed to us in the writings of God's revelation to his people. Where better, then to understand God, than to hear the Word read studied, prayed through, and hear the word preached diligently with eager desire as newborn babes? It is then,

---

[30] "...and to give you an inheritance among all them which are sanctified," (Acts 20:32).

[31] "But the hour cometh, and now is, when the true worshippers shall worship the Father in spirit and in truth: for the Father seeketh such to worship him," (John 4:23).

impossible to learn about God, or the Savior Jesus Christ, or the instrument of righteousness, the Spirit of Truth, without first understanding the Bible. Is that not a monumental, life-long task?

How might you discern God clearly in your daily devotions without understanding what the Bible says about God? How might you pray to a God you don't know? Or, know how to pray as God requires? How might you serve if you are not instructed as to serve in a certain capacity? How might you worship corporately if you do not know who God is, and what God desires in worship? And this is not accomplished on your own. This is integral as part of the common sanctification and growth of Christ's church towards biblical reformation. How do you contribute to the sanctification of Christ's church? Did you think sanctification was only individual? It is for *the body*. You are the body of Christ and each one of you is a part of it. What good would the hand do to grow strong if the arm was weak. What good would it be to learn something in your private devotions, only to keep it to yourself? You become robbers from others when you keep back what you learn in the word from others who are learning as well. Pastors in this light are professional encouragers and exhorters so to speak. What they have learned they share. What they know they share. This is applied to all, as we know and have heard already that we are to encourage one another while it is still called today. Holiness is individual, sanctification is individual, but it has a very corporate element to it. Do *you not want* to see everyone get to heaven? Do *you not want* to see everyone sanctified? These are the people you will spend eternity with. Is this important to you? You need their help and they need yours. God is not stingy with grace, neither should you be. We grow together, and we reform together. You may be the very means someone else is pressed further into the kingdom and sanctified. Now, this does not give you the right to be the holiness police; O! the danger of that for the wrong kind of A-type personality! This is when people want others to change but have no humility in expressing that, or that they fail to desire to really change themselves. Remember humility, encouragement, and consider others better than yourselves. Such an exhortation to help others to holiness can be a quick road of disaster to those who would exasperate others, or become like the one with a log in their eye trying to remove specks from others.[32] This all takes great wisdom, and a great amount of the Holy Spirit's direction, with age. Be the means in a most humble manner. Be ready to be used. God may just use you to help others.

With that said, be sure that you eagerly desire to grow by the pure milk of the word which is settled in a delightful experience towards biblical reformation. It is never your aim or goal to simply be in connection with the word, but it must affect you and change you and sanctify you. Tasting of the Lord, that he is good and

---

[32] Matthew 7:3ff.

kind to you, is an experimental connection and communion. Such a visit by God leaves in your soul a sweet remembrance of his presence. You *taste* it. The acts of the love of Christ showed to your soul when he visits you through the word, in the illumination of the Spirit, is increased by it. It leaves an impression of grace and holiness of God on your soul, like the fragrance of perfume from someone who has walked through the room recently. "I rose up to my beloved, and my hands dropped with myrrh, and my fingers with sweet smelling myrrh upon the handles of the lock," (Song of Solomon 5:5). Moses' meeting with God surrounding the Word of God, the Law in this case, left an impression of the glory of God on him. When he comes down from the mountain, he comes with his face shining. The bright beams of God's face are seen on his very face.[33] This is the experience of the Christian who dives deep into the word relying on the Spirit's illumination. Like babes they drink it up. And imagine if such communion was held by you all, all the time. That is what those sparks of revivals are made out of. But it cannot be forced, or manufactured. This is often a detriment to us. Trying to force something to happen because of knowledge. This growth would press all your souls after further fellowship and after further communion and after further spiritual growth, so that the desires of the whole

---

[33] "And the children of Israel saw the face of Moses, that the skin of Moses' face shone: and Moses put the vail upon his face again, until he went in to speak with him," (Exod. 34:35).

38

church are carried forth after greater and larger enjoyments of God through Christ. This is the heart of biblical reform. It is there, after higher and more glorious and fresh influences of the divine presence that you eagerly desire the pure milk of the word that you may grow thereby. And this leads one closer and closer to reformation of life.

Mark 2: Guarding the Heart and True Biblical Reform

(Take a moment to read Proverbs 4:10-27 with a focus on verse 23.)

"Keep thy heart with all diligence; for out of it are the issues of life," (Prov. 4:23).

While you are in the world, you must guard your heart. No biblical reformation will ever occur without this special guard on the heart. Lives are meant to be conformed to Jesus Christ.[1] Conforming to Christ is conforming to God's holy law. Keep in mind, reforming one's life may be a moral leap. A drunk may set themselves on the road of sobriety. A liar might start telling the truth. The addictive personality might throw off certain events and circumstances to be a better person. Yet, biblical reform in one's life is only accomplished, though, through rightly applying the Word of God. Reformation is always joined to a solemn resolve to continue to follow God's Word. True godliness and holiness only grow through the word, by the power of the Spirit.[2] Impiety will be suppressed. In what other way than by following God's word could one

---

[1] Rom. 8:29 and 12:2.
[2] "...but live according to God in the spirit," (1 Peter 4:6). "This I say then, Walk in the Spirit, and ye shall not fulfil the lust of the flesh," (Gal. 5:16).

grow in grace and sin be mortified? Holy lives are regulated by God's word in all things. In this, wise Christians are "doers of the Word," as the Apostle says.[3] They "observe to do," the Holy Spirit says. Christians never fail to receive what they sow by practice, and many times with increase as the Lord wills. The truth must be put into practice, and it is better than any stock or hedge fund, for it lies in God's promises that he will increase it by his Spirit.

True biblical reformation is always a thorough reform. It is *never* a partial reform in sincerity. Partial reformation is a partial forsaking of sin. Partial reformation is satisfied with a little grace. Partial reformation is not sincere. Partial reformation is a compromise. Partial reformation is only remembered by God in judgment. All of these are offensive to God. True Reformation envelops and involves the renewed Christian mind striving to become all that Christ desires it to be. "And be not conformed to this world: but be ye transformed by the renewing of your mind, that ye may prove what is that good, and acceptable, and perfect, will of God." (Rom. 12:2). That argues a change. It argues the need for a change.

Under Christ, *all* of life is to be reformed. The Lord Jesus will not be served with halves. Partial reformation is never something Christ is pleased with. He sees this as hypocrisy, which he abominates. He

---

[3] "But be ye doers of the word, and not hearers only, deceiving your own selves," (James 1:22).

requires all parts of all the lives of his servants. They are not allowed to keep any part back. It is all his, and it all tends to his glory; the church and it's worship, all the officers, and the congregation, the home, the federal husband, the industrious wife, the relationship between parents and children, the workplace, and even employers and employees. In these things Christians must make the most of every opportunity that is allotted to them toward reformation. They do this in the grace and power given to them by the Spirit of God. But how will this actually occur? What element is strewn throughout all these situations and places? It is the work of God on the heart.

Guarding the heart is a primary Spirit-empowered principle of the Christian walk. There must be a practical outworking as to how godly works come to pass, and that practical outworking will only be accomplished by guarding the heart from those things which would stop, reverse or distract the heart from making religion one's business.

Proverbs 4:23 is set in the greater context of the admonition of keeping to the right path. This proverb is written by Solomon, and set in the sayings of wisdom. If one wants to be wise, wise as the wisest man who may have ever lived, he would need to follow Solomon's great instruction in guarding the heart. It is a Christian's duty, and in it are the issues of life itself. We find here, that there are two paths to take. A person can resolve to walk a certain path and have good intentions, but practically, there is a way to go about making those resolutions come to pass, and there is another way to foul up one's life and so sin against God.[4] As seen every day in the world all around the Christian, take one path and it leads to moral depravity and eternal destruction, take another and it leads to happiness and eternal blessing. There are two paths, and only two, which are the choices God gives humanity. One is wide, and one is narrow.

Proverbs 4:10-27 envelops the larger context of various anatomical exhortations. There is a theology of walking set upon a right path. In this walking parts of the body are mentioned. The eyes are mentioned in v. 21 and 25. The mouth is mentioned in v. 24. The feet are mentioned in v. 26 and 27. The right path is seen and walked, but it is by determination, resolution, that it takes place. One path is light and life; everything else leads to darkness. The eyes, mouth, feet, all the members of one's body are to be used in righteousness because of a disposition of grace emitting and being cultivated in the heart. God put a principle of grace in the heart of the redeemed believer and that must be exercised and refined.

Proverbs 4:23 is crucial to taking the right path, for where the heart is, the rest of the body follows. "Keep" which may be better translated as guard, נָצַר (*natsar*) the Hebrew word meaning: to watch, guard,

---

[4] "Ponder the path of thy feet, and let all thy ways be established," (Prov. 4:26).

preserve from dangers with fidelity; guard as with a prison. What should be guarded?

"...Thy heart..." or the inner man, mind, will and understanding. It can also mean those parts coupled with the inclination, that which holds the power of *resolution*; a more modern way of saying this is that one has righteous determination of will. It is, in Scripture, the seat of the soul. The heart is the center or seat of man's being. It knows things. Proverbs 14:10, the heart knows its own bitterness, it has wisdom, Proverbs 14:33, for wisdom rests in the heart of him who has understanding. It is fallen in Adam and holds corruption. Jeremiah 17:9, "The heart is deceitful above all things, and desperately wicked; Who can know it?" It thinks, Matthew 15:19, "For out of the heart proceed evil thoughts." It is the seat of belief, Romans 10:10, "For with the heart one believes unto righteousness." It is the center of resolve in the verse at hand. Matthew 6:21, "For where your treasure is, there your heart will be also." As the heart is either pure or wicked, so is the whole course of a man's life. Out of the heart, from the heart, stem a great many things.

This heart is to be kept "...with all diligence..." literally, guarding the place of confinement, prison, guard, or jail house. This phrase is better translated with this idea: as a jailor watches the prisoner, and guards the prisoner in jail, so also the Christian is to guard the heart with a diligence or resolve in the same manner as confining criminals. One does not take that lightly. The heart of the Christian is criminal against God because of remaining sin, and continually attempts to overthrow any seeds of righteousness. While, at the same time, it has been renewed, and has a new principle of grace which gives the Christian the ability to guard it. Consider this idea like lockdown in a maximum security prison. What kind of thought and determination goes into how to hold criminals in such a foolproof facility, like Chateau D'if in the *Count of Monte Cristo*? It is interesting that the same Hebrew word used here is the same one used in Genesis 39:21-23 where Joseph is given authority *to keep* the prison. What would the thought process be to build a prison, a maximum security prison? Plans laid out, built, not out of straw like the little pig's house, but out of brick, steel, concrete, titanium? The right materials are needed. Even after this there would need to be a process put in place to tend the prison, feed the prisoners, keep them without harm, and such. There is a great strategy in all this.

What kind of strategy goes into guarding the heart? If prisons hold morally reprehensible and condemned prisoners, what supernatural agent will be used in guarding something supernaturally wicked and so intangible like a sinful heart. Or a heart in which one must guard as it relates to killing sin, and being transformed into something which resembles the Anointed Savior. Why is this *heart* so important? Solomon directs the reader: "For out of it spring the issues of life." Out of the heart comes forth everything that pertains to a person's life long path – all things regarding the manner and way of life. Above all things, this guarding is to be done. Nothing else good will come about in the life of the Christian who does not keep his heart. This "above all else" idea is linked to the tools that allow the Christian to guard the heart. This guard is a determining factor as to whether one is living righteously, or living wickedly. Christians, should, with all diligence, keep their hearts even though they cannot be completely free from sinful motions. Keeping the heart should be done as much as possible, for they are to keep themselves and guard themselves from all things which would encumber it as a command coming from Christ. They know they have the remnants of remaining sin in them, and if left unchecked, it will act like a snowball with sin, and make sin heavier for them. The way of his life comes out of his heart. Such a man who guards his heart before the face of God must have his life taken up with God. He looks to God as his Father, with Christ as his husband, the Spirit his mentor, and with the saints as his companions. If they do not guard it, if they are not exercised in it, such a negligent use of making the means of grace effectual to them will never occur. It causes them to be less fit to exercise and preserve divine and sanctifying motions from the Spirit of God.

The doctrine to consider here in light of biblical reformation is this, the practice of holy reform centers on guarding the heart with all diligence in Christ; above all else. Guarding the heart is a matter of life and death.[5] Out of the duty of doing this, or not, are, the issues of life. It is not good advice, not an easier path, or a simple change in a specific behavior that might be best. It's life and death. It is eternity in heaven or eternity in hell. Eternity is weighed in the balance. And God has, in his wisdom, set this duty on everyone. It is a *proverb*. Every person is made a guard of their heart; or at least should be. They are entrusted with a divine commission to be a guard. If they will not be their own guard in this way of the proverb, the world, the flesh and the devil have no problem stepping in to steal their hearts in a way contrary to God's direction. If their whole lives are not given over to Christ, and lived before Christ, and guided by Christ, the world and the flesh and the devil will certainly have no issue taking that responsibility over. Guarding is, in fact, in the greater context of *responsibility*. Without one keeping their heart, they will in fact not be able to fulfill what God says of keeping both themselves and others; there will be no biblical reformation at all. They are told to keep their heart, and then further, there is found the help and keeping of *others*. "Am I my brother's keeper?" (Gen. 4:9). Why *yes, you are*. And if the one is not keeping himself, how will he ever be able to aid a brother in need? Where will good advice come from? Where will that needed prayer come from?

---

[5] "See, I have set before thee this day life and good, and death and evil," (Deut. 30:15).

Life's issues flow from the heart that is to be guarded due to the matters of life and death. If those flowing rivers and streams are clear and good, the water is good to drink. But if the streams and rivers are polluted, where does one look to clean them up? It is at the source, the place where there are springs, or issues of life, it is there at the fountain, the heart. Joseph Hall said, "For, as the heart is the fountain of the natural life, so it is of the spiritual: there is the seat of grace and holiness: from there flows either the happiness or misery of man."[6]

Guarding the heart means there is something to guard against. The heart of a man, his will, mind and affections, are constantly barraged by evil desires opposite to the goodness and love of God. There must always be a sober watching and guarding against all those inlets that desire to take over the heart. "Be sober, be vigilant; because your adversary the devil, as a roaring lion, walketh about, seeking whom he may devour," (1 Peter 5:8). Hearts can be quickly devoured by the adversary if they are not guarded.

Guarding the heart presupposes that some kind of transformation has occurred so that the heart may be guarded. The wicked unregenerate heart is evil all the time. "Then the LORD saw that the wickedness of man was great in the earth, and that every intent of the thoughts of his heart was only evil continually," (Gen. 6:5). It is deceitful and desperately wicked, (Jer. 17:9). It

---

[6] Hall, Joseph, *The Works of Joseph Hall,* Volume 3, (Oxford: University Press, 1863) 240.

must be guarded, kept in check. Can guards in a prison take time off together with no one watching? Someone always has to be watching. Someone always must be at their post. What will the criminals do if the guards left the prison? To guard the heart means that God has graciously bestowed life in being born again from the Spirit, which in turn gives the sinner a new principle of grace in the heart, and new tools to exercise in their operation of divine instructions. Unless he has a new heart, he cannot guard his heart as God requires. He does not even know that he must guard the heart if he is unconverted.[7] This is the most difficult work that the Christian can engage in.

Guarding the heart holds in it a great duty for the Christian. To be *on guard.* To be *constantly at post.* What is worth protecting? Guarding the Heart is set over the entire life of the Christian – the issues of life. Banks have elaborate safes to protect money. Homes have alarm systems to protect valuables. People have insurance policies to protect their families. Guarding the heart holds a reason why the duty must be exercised, which is that all the matters of life, all things that matter, flow from it. To guard the heart holds in it the way the heart is to be guarded – with all diligence. How does one do this?

What does it mean to guard the heart? This means that the Christian has a constant, diligent

---

[7] "Because the carnal mind is enmity against God: for it is not subject to the law of God, neither indeed can be," (Rom. 8:7).

exercise and growth in all godly duties to preserve the soul against the evil of the day and sustain a holy relationship with Jesus Christ. There are two wonderful means by which the Christian may do this. The first powerful means is to understand what it cost to make atonement for that soul. The second is the right use of the word of God in its various ministries. Guarding the heart by a biblical understanding of the cost to make atonement for it. The best remedy for a slack heart, is to get to know the atonement of Christ more intimately, and God more exhaustively, and that, daily.[8] The most neglected topic in theology, in my estimation, is the Doctrine of God and Christ, and that is why most of the heresy that ruins the Christian walk falls around a misapprehension of who God is, what he is like, and what he has done through Christ on the cross. How would the Christian act differently about the nature of his heart, and its sanctification, or lack of it, if he were more intimately aware of the presence, holiness and character of God in his life, and cost of the only begotten Son of God? Guarding the heart is hard in this respect. Consider what God had to do through the Lord Jesus when he offered himself as a sacrifice for sin? Consider what Christ had to do as the sovereign Lord of life and death. The cross demonstrates the incomprehensible incarnation of the divine deity coming to earth to take on the flesh of men. Here, incarnate, walking in the

---

[8] "And not only so, but we also joy in God through our Lord Jesus Christ, by whom we have now received the atonement," (Rom. 5:11).

misery of the world, this God-man demonstrated the highest possible love of God for his people in living a life free from sin, and then willingly laid down His own life for sinners. He did not do this in some begrudging manner. It was done according to the joy set before him. He was not at fault, there was no sin in him; yet, the Lord was pleased to crush him, rendering him as a sin offering. What is man? What is sinful man, that God regards him in this way?

Christ is the Supreme Judge of all, the Son of Man, the divine being of heaven who cringed in the dust of Gethsemane casting himself before God with the most fervent prayers for deliverance, from the sentence of death and the curse of the law. Scripture says Christ, "...fell on his face, and prayed, saying, O my Father, if it be possible, let this cup pass from me: nevertheless not as I will, but as thou wilt," (Matt. 26:39). He sweat great drops of blood at the thought of it. "And being in an agony he prayed more earnestly: and his sweat was as it were great drops of blood falling down to the ground," (Luke 22:44). Before he went to the cross, he was already bleeding over it. Then he went to the cross: consider Pilate, the soldiers mocking and spitting, the crown of thorns, the purple robe, the nails and the wood and the screaming and the pain, and the seven sayings from the cross.

It was a great matter to make peace with God for sinners. It was a great matter to make atonement and reconciliation for sin for those who inherently deserved nothing. "But God commendeth his love toward us, in that, while we were yet sinners, Christ died for us," (Rom. 5:8). Such a daily contemplation of the excellence of seeing Christ so clearly in these things and an apprehension of what he endured for sin and the sinner, causes the Christian to be motioned by the Spirit to guard the heart with all diligence, for Christ died for this. Found in this work, in this cross of Christ, is the mystery of godliness. The whole business and duty of the Christian is linked to this mystery. "And without controversy great is the mystery of godliness: God was manifest in the flesh, justified in the Spirit, seen of angels, preached unto the Gentiles, believed on in the world, received up into glory," (1 Tim. 3:16).

Christ is the fountain and spring of grace,[9] and if that spring is found in the heart, then the heart is a fountain and spring of grace in the life of the believer. From that principle of divine grace in the heart spring forth the issues of life. From there more of Christ is brought forth. From there the Christian is conformed into holiness. It must be guarded as a treasure of infinite worth. Such guarding is moved and press by the most humble, holy and fruitful Christian, who is most diligent in guarding their heart, because they know what it cost God in the death of his Son to give them such a heart; this great spiritual mystery of the reconciliation of God

---

[9] "A fountain of gardens, a well of living waters," (Song of Solomon 4:15). God is "the fountain of living waters," (Jer. 17:13).

to sinners by the blood of the cross, and so they must always exercise faith in guarding it as most valuable.

Guarding the heart through the Word of God in its various ministries is crucial in all this. If Christ is set in the heart of a Christian, it will be a place of war. Satan, the world and the flesh will fight against Christ in the heart and the Word of God which directs him onto what path he is to take. "Your word I have hidden in my heart, That I might not sin against You!" (Psa. 119:11). The word is the great sword of the Spirit to vanquish sin and such. The Word of God protects the heart. How is walking the right path accomplished? Ephesians 5:17, "Therefore do not be unwise, but understand what the will of the Lord is." John Flavel said, "The keeping and right managing of the heart in every condition is the great business of a Christian's life."[10] They must know God's will in every condition, in every circumstance, for their whole life. Nehemiah 4:18, "Every one of the builders had his sword girded at his side as he built." They worked with the sword in one hand and the trowel in the other.

At what point can a Christian stop guarding his heart? There is hardship all around him in this fallen world. When does he get a break? You see then… Thomas Brooks said, "we should keep our hearts as under lock and key, that they may be always at hand when the Lord shall call for them."[11] Holding fast to the

---

[10] Flavel, John, *The Works of John Flavel*, Volume 10, (Carlisle, Banner of Truth Trust: 1995) 3.
[11] Brooks, Thomas, *The Works of Thomas Brooks*, Volume 3, (Carlisle, PA: Banner of Truth Trust, 1980) 385.

Word, and its memorization and incorporation is what sets the Christian on the Rock of Christ. Christ is the Living Logos - the Living Word. The Word of God, then, is hiding Christ in the heart for protection against the onslaught of the world, flesh and devil. God's Word is always under attack by the enemy. Genesis 3:1 records, "Now the serpent was more cunning than any beast of the field which the LORD God had made. And he said to the woman, "Has God indeed said, 'You shall not eat of every tree of the garden'?'" If the Word of God is set in the heart of a Christian, it will be a place of war. Satan, the world and the flesh will fight against the Word of God, fight against the life-principle of grace there, and fight against Christ himself, that is set in the Christian heart. They always have and always will until the end of the age.

Guarding the heart is no easy work, and yet, it must be a constant work because God's honor is on the line. God's honor is on the line when a Christian guards or does not guard his heart. What does the Christian attest to in his life and conversation? How does he live and what does he show men and God in that regard? In Hebrews 11:16 there is a very remarkable point on this to consider: "Therefore God is not ashamed to be called their God," (Heb. 11:16). In thinking about that verse, are there those that God is ashamed to be called their God? Are there Christians in which God is ashamed to be called their God because of their careless and negligent wayward life? I fear there may be. I fear they do not guard their heart as they should. God will be honored, as he does this in such a way as to pay every man his due. If a man dishonors God, God will dishonor him. Westminster Divine Francis Woodcock has an excellent work on 1 Samuel 2:30, "For them that honor me, I will honor; and them that despise me shall be lightly esteemed." He says, "God is specially regardful, and above all things tender, of his own honor."[12] Guarding or not guarding is to honor or not honor. The Christian should strive to fulfill the wisdom of Solomon in all this.

Consider all the wise strategy that goes into taking a terrorist city. The military, its leaders and their wisdom, the equipment and the billions upon billions of dollars which go into creating the most advanced technology, the training of all that equipment (training for ground incursion, missiles, tanks, air incursions, planes, specialized guns, missiles and such), the soldiering (learning how to be a good soldier), the commands which must be precisely followed, the timing, and such things. There is a lot that goes into conquering a terrorist city. Solomon also said, "He that ruleth his spirit, is better than he that taketh a city?" (Proverbs 17:2). Keeping the heart, guarding it effectively, is better than conquering a giant enemy city. The heart is such a small, little thing, but it holds in it, the issues of life and death. It is the rudder that steers

---

[12] Woodcock, Francis, *God Paying Every Man His Due, and Other Works*, (Crossville, TN: Puritan Publications, 2017) 20.

the ship. It is because for the Christian, Christ is found there in his action of keeping or not keeping his heart.

Guarding your heart depends on you continually protecting your heart in every condition from that which may corrupt it. Religion in this way, is your business; there is no reformation of life without it. You are required to do this continually (never stopping); you are on post and on point with the most solemn spiritual weapon, the sword of the Spirit, everyday of your whole life as a Christian. People who start businesses are very thorough to think through whether such a business succeeds or fails. What thought have you put into the strategy to guard your heart? "I'm going to guard my heart in this way...." and so you make an account of it.

Guard your heart by watching and guarding against all sin, generally speaking. It is a principle in our souls that presses us follow God, without which, we disregard what God says and do what *we* feel is best.

Avoiding sin. Avoid anything that would defile you. If you encounter sin, you have to resist it in its beginnings. You can't be knee deep in the mud and think you are going to overthrow sin easily.

If you fall into sin, repent quickly. Don't wait; Christ is a ready Savior to forgive, even 70 times seven.

Regulate your desires according to God's will. Know the word. Have high thoughts of God to further the motions of the Spirit once he is engaged with you. Practice having greater thoughts of him.

Pray to not only watch against sin in general, but sins that are particular to you. Particular besetting sins are very difficult to kill once they take hold. There is a great war and struggle in this that must be cast off.

Pray to be made aware of secret faults. These are those sins you do not even know you do. You are more apt to fall into those than public sins.

Consider that guarding our heart glorifies God in your sanctification and confirmation of Christ's image in you. As a Christian, you are stamped with the Holy Spirit of promise, that in his work and grace through you, your likeness to Christ might be more and more formed. Christ's perfections are mirrored by you. You reflect back to him his work in you. This is a great honor and privilege not given to every man or woman throughout the history of the created world. You are special in this; God chose you out of the world for this; he did not choose most people, but he chose you for it.

You are to be on guard, to guard that which is most valuable to God. The poorest Christian's heart is worth more than the riches of the whole world, or a million billion worlds put together. It concerns the issues of life and death. We are constantly under God's divine scrutiny in this.

Are we guarding our thoughts, actions, feelings, desires, intents, *etc.* Psalm 139:23 says, "Search me, O God, and know my heart; Try me, and know my anxieties." God is no doubt capable. Jeremiah 17:10, "I, the LORD, search the heart, I test the mind, Even to give every man according to his ways, According to the fruit of his doings." God looks at these things because he has paid a price for you in these things with the blood of his Son. He looks to increase in his investment in you. He looks to you to guard his spiritual portfolio in you. You must be on guard. Romans 8:13, "For if ye live after the flesh, ye shall die: but if ye through the Spirit do mortify the deeds of the body, ye shall live." Scripture is very black and white. Do this, and live, do this, and die. But guarding the heart is a full time work without any respite so that you can do this and live.

"We know that whoever is born of God does not sin; but he who has been born of God keeps himself, and the wicked one does not touch him," (1 John 5:18). You want to get radical with God in your sanctification and guard you heart in all safety? Spend a month reading 1 John each day. Every day for a month. See what changes occur in your devotional life from that study. Don't sin. Live holy. Honor God. Seek Christ. Walk in the light. Always believe. Keep his commandments. Love others. Be strong in the Lord. Reject evil. And that's just to chapter 2! Holiness is essential to success in life; holiness is the means to happiness (continually) and it is the center of biblical reformation.

If our minds are not wrapped around the concept of separation from the world and a separation and cleaving to God, then guarding the heart, or watching over it, will make little sense. What need is there to guard the heart if sin is not so bad? Sin is the evil of evils which caused the Christ to die on a cross. If you are a believer, he did this for you, in a most horrible way.[13]

Your knowledge of the Word is essential to success. Read your bible every day. If we desire biblical reformation in our home, work, church and society, then guarding our heart in light of Christ, by the power of the Word, is of prime importance. People say "doctrine is not important." Or sometimes, "too much doctrine is too much." But becoming more like Christ is only accomplished through the Word and we can never be enough in the Word or know the Word enough. Corrupt the Word or use of the Word and you corrupt the only means by which the Spirit sanctifies the soul. That is why Josiah tore his clothes after reading the book of the Law in 2 Kings. He knew he and all the people had fallen short of God's glory.

Without guarding our hearts safely, our hearts will be restless. Augustine said, "The soul is restless until it finds its rest in thee."[14] How will the heart or soul ever be ready for sanctification without guarding it? How will it ever endure a time of trial or mission if it is not properly watched? God will not mold clay that is not set on the potter's wheel. All the success of a holy life is set on whether or not the heart is filled with the Word of God, filled with Christ, and his work alone. To trust in his work and his life is the essence of Gospel belief.

---

[13] "And that he might reconcile both unto God in one body by the cross, having slain the enmity thereby," (Eph. 2:16).
[14] Lib 1,1-2,2.5,5: CSEL 33, 1-5.

Andrew Gray said, "Does God knock at your door by the ministry of His Word? Do not stop yours ears like the adder. Does He knock by the sweet inspirations of His Holy Spirit? You hear a voice behind you, saying, "This is the way, walk you in it?" Obey God's voice, and resolve presently, lest, death knocks suddenly at your door, and it be too late."

Be wise Christians.[15] God promises many great things to the heart that is guarded and engaged in Christian duties, the chief of which is wisdom. In Proverbs, just 4 chapters after we are pressed to guard our heart, wisdom shouts and beckons you to be *wise* Christians. "I love those who love me, and those who seek me diligently will find me." (Prov. 8:17). Again, diligently. Prepared. Strategic. Ready. Empowered. These kinds of words go together. What does the careless heart lose?

Ask yourself, "Can I stir up my affections to get my heart right with God, that I might obtain mercy which would last into eternity?" This is where you make religion your chief business, and you engage in guarding your heart before God. You will never have an iota of conformity to Christ with a careless heart. The Christian must guard his heart in order to rightly honor the Lord Jesus. These are not secondary issues. They are issues of life and death. For, the practice of holy reform and

---

[15] "See then that ye walk circumspectly, not as fools, but as wise, redeeming the time, because the days are evil," (Eph. 5:15-16).

biblical reformation center on guarding your heart with all diligence, above all else.

Mark 3: Rejecting Partial Reformation as Sin and a Full Offense to God

"Ephraim, he hath mixed himself among the people; Ephraim is a cake not turned," (Hosea 7:8).

We find in Hosea 7 Ephraim's sin. There is recorded there the church's apostasy through Ephraim. God's case here is against Ephraim who mixed the church with the world. The former two chapters were against Judah, but now God turns to Ephraim and shows the waywardness of the church in false worship. God's central message here is about spiritual adultery.

Gomer and Hosea are used as illustrations of God's rescuing his people from idolatry, which point to God's faithfulness as the husband, and the church's unfaithfulness with its wandering eyes toward sin. In the first chapters of the prophet's book, Hosea's wife Gomer has that wandering adulterous eye, one that must be rescued by the faithful husband. This is only accomplished by Christ, though seen here in this book in various types and shadows. In chapter 7, the illustration changes somewhat, where the adulterous woman and husband, now become a patient and doctor. God is the healer, who would have healed his people if they would simply hear and hold steadfastly to the word. "When I would have *healed* Israel." Ephraim and

Samaria are called out as being the "snake's head" of this sin of compromise; a mixing.

"The iniquity of Ephraim is uncovered, And the evil deeds of Samaria, for they deal falsely; the thief enters in, Bandits raid outside, and they do not consider in their hearts that I remember all their wickedness. Now their deeds are all around them; they are before My face," (Hosea 7:1-2). The leaders of the people were not doing what they should be doing before God, not attending their duties faithfully before God, both at home and in corporate worship. Their wickedness in not being holy as God requires is seen as walking before God's face. They are at fault for not considering these important spiritual duties as God so lays them out. They believe that they determine what is acceptable and what is not. But true religion is no democracy. They have mixed true religion with the world. "They make a king glad with their wickedness, and princes with their lies," (Hos. 7:3). They make the earthly king glad by their submission to false worship and false walking before God's face.

Under the king and the changes made to God's worship by Jeroboam at this time, the leaders wondered how the people would react. Would the people be angry with them for changing God's worship? Or would they be in agreement? So, when the king saw that the changes made to worship were pleasing to the people, the king rejoiced. Wicked people are always easily led into apostasy by wayward leaders. Ephraim allowed worldly influences into the worship and life of the church. Foreign gods, foreign to God in idolatry; all this was spiritual adultery.

"In the day of our king Princes have made him sick, inflamed with wine; He stretched out his hand with scoffers," (Hos. 7:5). The people *rejoiced* in the day of the king who set up false worship and idolatry. You see, they no longer had to travel to the temple to worship, having to traverse dangerous roads and bandits through Samaria in that day. They were happy that the king had overridden God's prescription of holiness to do something *different*. The king made worship easier and more palatable. He made it simpler; *different*, by mixing it with the world. The heinousness of the sin is also heightened by a festival day. It was the "day of our king" or, his birthday. They made him drunk with wine, and the text refers to the king being indisposed by his wicked mind as to party with scoffers against true religion.

Then, God, very graphically, gives an illustration of a baker. The illustration shifts yet again. "For they have made ready their heart like an oven, whilest they lie in wait: their baker sleepeth all the night; in the morning it burneth as a flaming fire. They are all hot as an oven, and have devoured their judges; all their kings are fallen: there is none among them that calleth unto me," (Hos. 7:6-7). They are passionate for the wrong things. Their hearts are prepared, readied, set, to *change* worship. How do they do it? Jesus said, beware of the leaven of the Pharisees.[1] Paul exhorted, "A little leaven leaveneth the whole lump," (Gal. 5:9). The illustration of a baker is quite appropriate. And then, the baker, after leavening his lump and preparing it quickly, falls asleep and goes to bed heating up his oven for the morning. They have an oven, a baker, food to cook, a fire stoked. They have *done* much. But they have not done enough because they have changed their walk and worship into a lie. Mix a drop of poison into a fresh glass of water, and it makes it poison. It's no longer drinkable. Like the leaven of the Pharisees, Jesus says, *beware.*

Religious leaders are charged with the preservation of righteousness and holiness for the people in worship and for life and godliness.[2] People are charged with holding leaders accountable to God's prescription for holiness if they become wayward. On both accounts Ephraim failed miserably. Likened to a baker, zealous and hot for their own recipe, ready to bake cakes but falling asleep, they committed spiritual adultery and reveled in it.

"They are all hot, like an oven, and have devoured their judges; All their kings have fallen. None among them calls upon Me," (Hos. 7:7). False worship setting itself from the king downward, devours all those in authority because they abdicate their authority by changing what God requires in life and worship. God

---

[1] Matt. 16:6, 11-12; Mark 8:15; Luke 12:1.
[2] "For the priest's lips should keep knowledge, and they should seek the law at his mouth: for he is the messenger of the LORD of hosts," (Mal. 2:7).

says all their kings are fallen. All those who would lead them in religious truth are fallen. "Fallen from grace," (Gal. 5:4). "Remember therefore from whence thou art fallen," (Rev. 2:5). God also makes a note, that even in the midst of whatever they are doing in their false worship, none of them calls on him. One cannot call on God falsely; or, when they are sleeping. Even when one calls on God, if they do it falsely, it is both as if they did not do it at all, and did something contrary to God's will.

Then comes the judgment. Ephraim is like a cake not turned. "Ephraim has mixed himself among the peoples; Ephraim is a cake not turned," (Hos. 7:8). The wickedness of their sin is commented on in 2 Kings 17:33, "They feared the LORD, yet served their own gods according to the rituals of the nations from among whom they were carried away." When did they make the church like the world? "They made Jeroboam the son of Nebat king. Then Jeroboam drove Israel from following the LORD, and made them commit a great sin. For the children of Israel walked in all the sins of Jeroboam which he did; they did not depart from them," (2 Kings 17:21-22). Ephraim, the church, is representative, the head of the snake, so to speak, in this false worship and idolatry following Jeroboam's treacherous wickedness. They mixed God's worship with idolatry, changed God's prescription for worship to the superstitions of foreign nations.

What does it mean that they are a cake not turned? It means they are half baked. Not acceptable food; burned on one side and raw on the other. Useless and good for, literally, *nothing*. It did not matter to them to worship or live falsely. The worship of God was corrupted and all their sacrifices were adulterated. All of the godliness of true religion was a confused mess. They were *content* to be idolaters. They did have some good worship practices. It was not *all* false. It was *mixed* with false. One side of the cake started out good. Doesn't that make it edible? No. Such a position is false, for a half truth is a whole lie. On this text, Jeremiah Burroughs rightly said, "Idolatry and superstition are the grey hairs of a dying condition."[3]

Consider that partial reformation is a full offense to God, a cake not turned. No matter how satisfied a church might be in their personal course of reform, and no matter how much true reform may be mixed with that which is false, if it is but partial, it is all offensive to God. Does that seem harsh? *God was the one who said it.* Such churches are with Ephraim a cake not turned, in God's eyes, *good for nothing.* With the wave of compromise in the church today, this text ought to be horrifying to Evangelical America.

Partial Reformation is offensive to God because partial idolatry is *always* full idolatry. The devil and his minions are out to twist and destroy the life and worship of the church. He has very cunning plans. The church is

---

[3] Burroughs, Jeremiah, *An Exposition of the Prophecy of Hosea*, (Edinburgh: J. Nichol, 1863) 343.

not to be unaware of his devices.[4] Today, most Christians couldn't name one device. The church has need to look to their ways. But Ephraim was so sincere! Sincerity in transgression against God is still sin.

Partial reformation in conversion and sanctification are both sins. In conversion it is much like the words of Augustine when he said, "Give me chastity, but not yet." That is akin to, "I want to change, and change a little, but not in every area." Good intentions falling short are not real.

What is a partial conversion? What is partial reformation in conversion? How can partial anything be a full anything? Think of the doctrine of repentance – is repentance just confession of sin? No. It relies, first, on the principle of grace. The Spirit of Grace must first do a supernatural work in a person[5] before acceptable repentance through Christ is even possible. "Unless a man is born again he *cannot...*" Repentance is sight of sin, sorrow for sin, confession of sin, shame of sin, hatred of sin, and turning from sin. It is not just one ingredient in baking that cake. And no doubt, in the way sinners repent, even their repentance often needs repenting of. What part of repentance, what part of conversion can be partial? Partial conversion or partial reform in this way is an oxy-moron. What of comparing partial reform in

---

[4] "Lest Satan should get an advantage of us: for we are not ignorant of his devices," (2 Cor. 2:11).
[5] "Jesus answered and said unto him, Verily, verily, I say unto thee, Except a man be born again, he cannot see the kingdom of God," (John 3:3).

sanctification and being more holy? This speaks closer to the idea presented in the text. Could good king Josiah in his *full-reformation* say, "Lord, I want to have right worship, but I am going to skip fixing the temple, or cleaning out the pagan artifacts within it. I am only going to take care of some things, but not all things. I am not resolved to take care of it all, but only some of it." Churches say, "We want biblical worship, we want holy lives, (what great intentions) but let us add in puppet shows and parades so that we can attract more people to the church and make it entertaining, and let us forsake the Lord's Day or family worship and we will be happy – because a little reform is better than nothing." The mixing of worldliness of this kind has always been the downfall of the church. This is because God regulates how worship should be maintained, not men, and men are prone to unbelief. *God* determines how sinners approach him, not *sinners*. Reformation only occurs by the direction of the Word – by a solemn oath to the Word and to God – and with a thorough resolve.

Hypocrisy is always against biblical reformation. It is saying with one side of the mouth that one upholds the Bible, and with the other it violates biblical Principles or shows forth an inconsistent life before the face of God. That is not reformation – it is compromise and hypocrisy. That is a cake not turned. And this is because partial reform is *always* a full offense to God.

The question is: why? Why is a partial reformation fully offensive to God? It is seen in five ways.

[1] It is a partial forsaking of sin; coming short of God's requirements and law, which is offensive to God. Churches and Christians often think that some partial reformation is sufficient, and if they are reformed a little in this or that particular thing, then everything is good. They think, "we have enough and that is what counts, for if we are reformed a little, we can use the word "reformed" in our church name! Better to have a little, or partial, or some reform, then none at all, isn't it? That's really arguing a better degree of *apostasy*. This degree of apostasy is better than that degree of apostasy, isn't it? Why not use *that* term? They then should label their church as the *first apostate church of such and such a city*. They think all will be well with them if they at the very least, in some way, mirror the truth *partially*; they are, in fact, only human, right? When a drunk man becomes sober he thinks he is a new man. Is he? Is carnal sobriety for a moment true reformation? Check him out in a day or two, or a week or two, you will find him a recovering *drunk*. But, at least he's sober part of the time, right? If a wicked person makes the leap to be a bit more moral, does that argue being born by the Spirit? He is not in total corruption as he was before. Maybe he is a better worker at work, or argues for being a better husband, or a friendlier neighbor. Does that really give him full reformation of life? Thomas Watson said, "Some leave drunkenness, and live in covetousness; they forbear swearing, and live in slandering. It is but a partial

reformation, and so they miss the kingdom of glory."[6] When a church or Christian in a church believes that a partial forsaking of some sin is acceptable before God, they think that the vital principle of holy zeal in reformation is unnecessary. If a little is enough, then the full weight of the Spirit of God working toward sanctification is not really necessary.

Now, it is wholly another thing to say, not everyone is sanctified at the same time and in the same degree. But degrees of sanctification do not argue the neglect of the principle; to be sanctified in the whole man. But satisfaction with a little reform is far different than this. With Ephraim, it translated straightway into false living and false worship. When worship is only somewhat false, is that acceptable to God or is it offensive to him? Some would say, but the church has to start somewhere, right? No, no, the church must start and begin and run and end everywhere as God prescribes. Otherwise, God sees it as wholly offensive. ""But if there is a defect in it, if it is lame or blind or has any serious defect, you shall not sacrifice it to the LORD your God," (Deut. 15:21), like a cake not turned. Did Christ come and die for a partial forsaking of sin? "Pursue ... holiness, without which no one will see the Lord: looking carefully lest anyone fall short of the grace of God," (Heb. 12:14-15). Not partial holiness, or some holiness or a little holiness. Set in the context of the

---

[6] Watson, Thomas, *The Lord's Prayer*, (Edinburgh: Banner of Truth Trust, 1993) 109.

faithful High Priest, the Anointed Savior, people are to repent and do the works worthy of repentance; are they only required to do this partially? Is Christ OK in his complete work with a partial reformation of someone's life? With a church partially reformed? Is that where it ends?

Partial reform can never lie in moral righteousness. "For I say to you, that unless your righteousness exceeds the righteousness of the scribes and Pharisees, you will by no means enter the kingdom of heaven," (Matt. 5:20). Does God accept partial morality? The Pharisees did many things that they should have done, yet, they were partial in their reform.[7] *Beware of the leaven of the Pharisee.* What about one's religious life? It includes moral righteousness. It is not merely some external conformity to part of what God says. Do men sometimes have a form of godliness yet deny its power?[8] Yes, very often. How often is this actually applied to Christians who have a partial reform and leave it at that? Having a form of godliness, but denying its power denies God. It involves only partial humiliation, partial illumination, partial conviction, partial reformation. Partial things *apostates* can do. Like Ephraim, they are a cake not turned. An apostate may be enlightened, (Heb. 6:4). Does Felix truly tremble under conviction before Paul in being *almost* a Christian? How

---

[7] "...these ought ye to have done, and not to leave the other undone," (Matt. 23:23).

[8] 2 Tim. 3:5.

close to the Kingdom is almost? Partial reformation of life and worship is offensive to God and it is like a cake not turned.

[2] Partial reformation is satisfied with just a little grace. Partial reformation does not want full reform, but to be content with a little religiosity. The 21st Century Church is willing to part with some particular sins, while they indulge others, that by this partial reformation they may free themselves in their conscience from the condemning sentence of the law. Whatever purposes or feeble efforts they may make towards reformation, because they think a little is better than nothing, they bring no fruit to perfection, but remain deprived of every degree of walking with God which he requires. Why? Because partial reformation is fully offensive to God. The church can never be contented with a little grace, a little religion, a little piety, a little worship, a little prayer, a little sanctification. Where does God ever tell his people to do *just a little.* God requires his people to take the kingdom by violence. He requires them to take it by force.[9] They are clothed in armor to fight, with no armor for retreating on their back.[10] They are always engaged, always pressing into the kingdom,[11] always moving forward. Or they are on the road of apostasy. Where

---

[9] "And from the days of John the Baptist until now the kingdom of heaven suffereth violence, and the violent take it by force," (Matt. 11:12).
[10] Eph. 6:11ff.
[11] Luke 16:16.

does Scripture ever tell them to be contented with just a little sanctifying power?

[3] Partial reformation is not sincere. There are myriads of denominations and churches that will gladly say "we hold to the Bible and the Westminster Confession," but are filled with *exceptions.* They only hold to such things partially. What does it mean to live in accordance with God's word sincerely and fully? Free from the pretense of hypocrisy. Partial reform is by nature contrary to God's prescription of holiness and worship and is therefore insincere and hypocritical. It is like saying, "I love you Lord, but..." Reform is a reformation from sin and wickedness of all kinds; because turning from sin is comprehensive. "Through Your precepts I get understanding; Therefore I hate *every* false way," (Psa. 119:104). Partial reformation shows that one only hates some false ways and allows others. It is content with a little. In contrast, "Grace be with all those who love our Lord Jesus Christ in sincerity," (Eph. 6:24). This is in purity, without corruption, perpetually. Thomas Boston said, "God requires the whole heart and he will not be served in halves."[12] Such a partial reform of life and worship would be insincere, like a cake not turned.

[4] Partial reformation is a compromise. God's prescriptions are offensive to the natural man. Churches filled with unregenerate people will hate godly worship.

---

[12] Boston, Thomas, *The Complete Works of Thomas Boston*, Volume 6, (Wheaton: Richard Owen Roberts Publishers, 1980) 421.

Worship, as with Ephraim, will then be made more palatable; made easier and more attractive. In that, God's worship is rejected, and something new is set in its place. Compromise – to accept standards that are lower than God has prescribed. Partial reformation leans in the direction of compromise, and it looks for the approval of the natural man; or, in the approval of the professing believer who has been deceived to sin, to make worship more palatable. Compromise caters to the carnal mind. Compromise shows one's sinful desires. With Ephraim through Jeroboam this was not only the case, but verses 1-3 and 8 speak directly to it. They pleased men, and compromised their worship, moving away from God's prescription, having a form of godliness, denying true power, and becoming adulterers. "They are all adulterers. Like an oven heated by a baker..." (Hosea 7:4). That's *God* speaking. They stoke the fire of their passion, God says, and they go to sleep waiting for the fire to be as hot as it needs to be for their recipe and their negligent cooking. In the morning the baker finds his oven well heated, and ready. These wicked people, having laid their lusts counter to the prescription of God, have their hearts so fully set in them to do evil that, the lust in their heart is like fire in a heated oven. They don't even cook well. Their food is half baked. And they go about their business at the expense of God's will. In doing so, they are like a cake not turned.

[5] Partial reformation is never remembered by God for good, but only in judgment. God never says,

anywhere in Scripture, it's good that you worship me in spirit, but not in truth. It's good you do some things, so I'll over look the other things that you have left off. He never concedes an iota or a jot, or a tittle. "For assuredly, I say to you, till heaven and earth pass away, one jot or one tittle will by no means pass from the law till all is fulfilled. Whoever therefore breaks one of the least of these commandments, and teaches men so, shall be called least in the kingdom of heaven," (Matt. 5:18-19). He never concedes that a little is acceptable. He never concedes that some reform is better than none so that makes everything fine. In previous chapters of Hosea, God said of Ephraim, "Ephraim is joined to idols, Let him alone." (Hos. 4:17). Don't pray for him, don't intercede, don't interfere. Not even the means of grace at this point do them any good. What a woeful place to be! None of their worship does them any good? All their supposed false sincerity in partial reformation does them *no good*. God *pays them no mind*. They still have their church, and their events, and their mid-week meetings, and their age-specific gatherings, and their street evangelism day, and their potlucks, and such, but *God is not there* for he sees them as a cake not turned.

A very interesting rebuke is given by the prophet Ezekiel, "When I say to the righteous that he shall surely live, but he trusts in his own righteousness and commits iniquity, none of his righteous works shall be remembered; but because of the iniquity that he has committed, he shall die," (Ezek. 33:13). Matthew Henry said in his commentary on the prophet Hosea concerning these verses, "Those who think to cheat God by dissembled repentance and partial reformation, put the greatest cheat upon their own souls."

The serious nature of partial reformation and the obstacles to Christ's spiritual benefits is glaring in all of this. When God instructs the church to reform, whether in chastisement or in benefits, the church should receive him as he proposes; on his terms. What a glorious thing it is for Christ to come in his humiliation to save us, or even in his anger to correct us. In either, the church should embrace him. In worship, all that is done without God's Word, is doing we do not know, as Christ says in John 4:22 "You worship you know not what." But what does the church do when God comes to rescue them? Do they instantly become better cooks? Do they attend faithfully that station on the cooking line for dinner, to press the illustration? This is what he requires.

The great hindrance to full reformation over partial reformation is the lack of godly conviction in the truth and, as a result, *people of the world* are leading the church instead of the Scriptures. It always seems like there are relatively few people stirring the pot against the overwhelming majority who desire to do things differently; much like a Hosea to Gomer, or God to Ephraim. Are there so many learned and wise professors and theologians today and confessional preachers who don't mind a cake not turned? Are there not so many people who rise up against all this? Martin Luther said that this was a great temptation to him, "Are you alone wise, are all others in an error?" What would the reformation have done if Luther had given in to his temptations not to fully reform? What kind of reformation would occur if Christ gave into such things in his earthly ministry among the Pharisees and temple robbers? Jesus always did everything to the greatest degree. It was said of the Savior, "The zeal of thine house hath eaten me up," (John 2:17). Churches today have zeal for their own agendas, and care little about true reformation. Edmund Calamy said, "Always, reformations have been judged impossible things."[13] But, it is far better to endure contempt by compromising *Jereboams* in the church then the anger of God; better to have the entire world despise the people of God, then God frown on professing disciples who do not walk in his way. Better to be frowned on and an edible cake, rather than, like Ephraim, a cake not turned, good for nothing.

What is the usefulness of a cake not turned? People in the contemporary Evangelical church *hope* to have a good relationship with God by a partial reformation. They think this way along with those whose hearts are unhumbled and unchanged. The sinner who is lost and without the Lord Jesus Christ hopes for much the same. They hope God will be gracious to them

---

[13] Calamy, Edmund, and C. Matthew McMahon, *Gradual Reformation Intolerable*, (Coconut Creek, FL: Puritan Publications, 2014, Second Edition) 100.

today. They hope they have done enough good things to outweigh their bad things today. They hope to obtain some of the benefits Christ offers in their worship of him. They might even expect not to receive all of them because they know they are not perfect. That is false humility if it is not connected with reformation.

What does God think when they only pursue part of what he says while leaving off the rest? The problem the evangelical reformed church has is that it looks at these important issues of sanctifying righteousness and worship before God as his people *from a human perspective.* Isn't it better to compromise the worship of the church to attract more people so we tell them about the Gospel and they can be saved? They do not consider that "in vain do they worship" Christ, teaching for doctrines the commandments of men.[14] The reformation of the church never consists in bringing-in new doctrines or new changes. It consists in reform by casting them out and trimming them off. Reform argues loving the old paths.[15]

The reception of the old paths that lead to godliness are the hallmarks of every reformation. Consider Cain in Genesis 4 that "If thou doest well, shalt

---

[14] "But in vain they do worship me, teaching for doctrines the commandments of men," (Matt. 15:9).
[15] "Thus saith the LORD, Stand ye in the ways, and see, and ask for the old paths, where is the good way, and walk therein, and ye shall find rest for your souls. But they said, We will not walk therein," (Jer. 6:16).

thou not be accepted?"[16] This was directly related to *worship.* He killed his brother over his envy of Abel's acceptable worship and his rejected worship. How many evangelicals today will be told the same? These kinds of false leaders follow Cain's example. They stone people theologically in their congregations. When God redeemed the Israelites into the wilderness "to worship him" he did not tell them to take a poll or to check with others as to what they might do to be acceptable worship. He gave them specific instructions to follow. Nadab and Abihu were killed for not heeding that in Leviticus 10.[17] When Josiah had his Reformation, they followed the book of the law, not in part but in whole, they took a stand in the covenant. In Ezekiel's vision in chapter 8 God is displeased with those who in the "chambers of imagery," worship falsely, both in the dark at home and then what they bring of that to church, "in vain imaginations" in "will-worship" worship. They worshipped God according to their own vain imaginations.

You might think, "What you are proposing is impossible for human beings to do, so, we cannot be required by such high standards." That kind of argument

---

[16] "If thou doest well, shalt thou not be accepted? and if thou doest not well, sin lieth at the door. And unto thee shall be his desire, and thou shalt rule over him," (Gen. 4:7).

[17] "And Nadab and Abihu, the sons of Aaron, took either of them his censer, and put fire therein, and put incense thereon, and offered strange fire before the LORD, which he commanded them not. And there went out fire from the LORD, and devoured them, and they died before the LORD," (Lev. 10:1-2).

is a great historical deception; it's *devilish*. God requires his church to act and work in a particular way; by his prescription. Should professing Christians not act in accordance with it, be happy with part of the work done, because a little is better than none at all? But annexed to this is the Spirit who produces the fruits of righteousness in his church. If there is no fruit, no fruit by the Spirit in this way, then the tree is bad. Christ says it is good for nothing but to be cut down and thrown into the fire and burned.[18] How many filled churches are thrown on this theological fire? There is a difference between doing the right things in a weak or imperfect way, and doing the wrong things above, over and against what God has said. Imperfection in doing what is right as a redeemed sinner, if righted by Christ's imputed righteousness, is acceptable to God. God accepts your right worship, though it is weak, because you bring Christ in it. But doing that which God never prescribes, or is just plain wrong, is judged according to Christ's righteous prescription. Doing what God does not prescribe, and doing what God requires are two *very different things*.

---

[18] "And the people shall be as the burnings of lime: as thorns cut up shall they be burned in the fire," (Isa. 33:12). "As therefore the tares are gathered and burned in the fire; so shall it be in the end of this world," (Matt. 13:40). "If a man abide not in me, he is cast forth as a branch, and is withered; and men gather them, and cast them into the fire, and they are burned," (John 15:6).

What if the church does not heed the voice of the Shepherd?[19] God desires his church to respect his threatenings, and give him the worship he desires in daily life and church practice. It is a terrible sign when the people of a church, or leaders of a church, "refuse to hearken," draw "away the shoulder," and "make their heart as an adamant; lest they should hear the law, and the words" of God by the truth, Scripture says. Zechariah said that and continues in 7:11-12 and says, "Therefore came a great wrath from the Lord of hosts." Romans 1 says that such a wrath that God brings is often by way of giving them over to themselves. Like Ephraim joined to idols. Regardless of how God's threatenings come, by the mouths of his ministers, or rebukes from people, or simply from some conviction by the word through the Spirit, to disregard them sears the consciences of people. "Break up your fallow ground, and sow not among thorns," (Jer. 4:3).

The global evangelical church today sows among the thorns in this; it *plants thorns*. The heart prepared by God for a full reformation, a true one, "Sows to yourselves in righteousness," so, return to God in sincerity and be "trees of righteousness." (Isa. 61:3). Ephraim was hammered by God and abandoned because they hammered out idols of their own making. You in the church are to persist in this work of worship and sincerity of walking before God until you find his favor,

---

[19] "To him the porter openeth; and the sheep hear his voice: and he calleth his own sheep by name, and leadeth them out," (John 10:3).

even "till he comes and rains righteousness upon you." John Willison said, "There is a natural popery in the minds of men; fallen man is desirous to stand upon his own feet, and is as little content with God's judgments of things as his first parent was in paradise. We are studious of making God compensations, applauding ourselves in our own inventions and satisfactions of our own minting, unwilling to acquiesce in his wisdom. This is a high presumption."[20]

If Christ is the perfect Mediator and Sacrifice for his people, and he alone prescribes the manner in which sinners approach him in life and worship, in full reform of their sinful course to sanctifying righteousness, it is a boldness and blasphemy in us not to think the same way. Can we pretend to do anything other than what God has instructed, without charging him with weakness and deficiency? Is his divine will not enough to make his directions complete, without some extras added in from our corrupt humanity? Do we have to think something must come from us to strengthen God's prescription for life and godliness? All who do this makes Scripture to be a lie, when Heb. 10:14 says, "by one offering he has perfected forever them that are sanctified." So, to make Christ a Savior in part, is to make him no Savior. All these kinds of additions and subtractions to worship and walking in the Spirit sinfully presume on the honor of Christ's completed

---

[20] Willison, John, *The Whole Works of the Rev. and Learned John Willison*, (Edinburgh: J. Pillans and Son, 1816) 184.

work. It is to pull the crown off Christ's head and set it on our own head. It is the highest foolhardiness to add or subtract to the life and worship that God has instructed his people to obey or to add to in the way of walking like a true Christian. What can man offer in wisdom to God that can be in any way equivalent to what God has already established? It is a very desperate thing to refuse God's will, a will which is so sweet to him. Partial reformation is a great and heinous sin in this light. It tramples on that which is God's delight; which is his own will. Such change to what God has established is nothing more than unbelief. It is the language of an unbeliever's heart.

God never blesses a cake not turned. He is not in nor blesses any of those compromises. Anything he has not prescribed, anything not set down by his own will, he has nothing to do with. But, the argument goes, there are so many people in such and such a church, or in such and such a denomination; *surely* God is blessing it. *Surely* God is in it. Christ calls such things "vain worship." Paul calls it "will worship."[21] The natural man is so easily pleased with the things of the world, and when the church looks like the world it will attract so many people, and it will engage in so many compromising works.

---

[21] "Which things have indeed a shew of wisdom in will worship, and humility, and neglecting of the body; not in any honour to the satisfying of the flesh," (Col. 2:23).

Now, at that point, many will be saying amen, and agreeing, and such; "O! yes, we must have God as our God as he is so prescribed." But let's merely take the example of worship and remove the shadows of the temple from the evangelical church today: when I say that special music has no place in the worship service, solos are out, choirs are out, worship by proxy is out, instruments in worship are out, guitars and pianos and such, parades in the church are out, mime is out, and interpretive dance is out, skits are out, orchestras are out, worship teams are out, uninspired hymns are out, and any resurrection of Old Testament Temple worship *is out*, people are suddenly going to have a far different thought about that. Oh, they don't want those things out. They *like* those things. It makes worship more palatable. And there it is, at that point, they reject the biblical principle of God's worship just like Ephraim did and they are happy to do so; they'll even throw a potluck party for it.

Is this not the meaning behind the text? They want all those things indifferently because they like them. God says that such things are a cake not turned; useless and good for nothing. Jesus said, no more temple worship (John 4:23-24). Why would one want to go back and walk back behind the veil in worship? The reason is because they like it; it is excitingly filled with pomp and circumstance. Yet, it is idolatry of the highest order according to Jesus' prescription for worship in John 4; and do not mistake it, God is in *none* of those things; nor does he bless those things no matter how sincere people are or how many people are sitting in the pew. To partially worship God and mix men's imaginations into it, is to forsake him. *You are cakes not turned who do so.*

Imagine if Christ did the same with salvation and that he only partially saved? Some people only want a partial reform in their church worship, in their house, in their family, in their life, because partial is better than nothing, humanly speaking, so they say. You even hear some preachers and godly men who are trying to reform the church say, "Oh, we can't have all we desire (even if they did desire the full reform God is speaking of here), so part is better than nothing." Let's have *that* conversation face to face with God. "You know Lord, we decided among ourselves, because not everyone was on board, that it was better for your church just to do some of the things you commanded for life and godliness and leave others off, and we also added in what we liked and took out some things that would hinder people from coming to our church; I mean, Lord, we just added a little bit of the world." "I'm steadfast," they say, "I uphold the faith while being part of this or that denomination, I hold to the truth and I'm trying to change what is going on there." But God says, after so many tries, *Ephraim is joined to idols, leave him alone.* God is not there, and so what strides will be made? Metaphorically speaking, burn it down and start over.

Do you work partially at work; see what that gets you. Love your family partially? Love your wife or husband partially? Love your children partially? Mow your lawn partially? Do you do anything partially in that way that you deem important or necessary? If Christ was only a partial Savior what a horror that would be? Churches would then rest in the discernment of fallen men to decide what spiritual things should be done and accomplished for God's glory if Jesus did not do all God wanted him to do. Men would have to make up the difference. What kind of odd things would one find in a church that thought that way? Imagine if he only saved you from half your sins. Which half? What would you do to rid yourself of the other half? Imagine if Christ only gave you some of the Spirit, or only on special occasions? Left to yourselves the rest of the time. There are myriads of churches that practically think that way. If they don't say it that way, they practically live it out that way. They are a cake not turned.

Or they go to the other extreme and say it doesn't matter what we do because Jesus will forgive and save us anyway. No, God never gives us the excuse of being law-less (without his law and prescription for the way of holiness) and there is no room in Christianity for such presumption. Jesus is not an *indifferent Redeemer*. He is not apathetic to how his mystical body acts and lives and worships him. Jesus said, "And then will I profess unto them, I never knew you: depart from me, ye that work iniquity," (Matt. 7:23). He is a full Savior, a complete Savior who hates even the idea of partial reform; he wants full reformation in the hearts of all his people, and he will have it by the power of the Spirit in the faithful elect. He says to compromising churches and denominations, "I know your works, that you are neither cold nor hot. I could wish you were cold or hot. So then, because you are lukewarm, and neither cold nor hot, I will vomit you out of My mouth," (Rev. 3:15-16). He abominates cakes not turned. He throws them up because they are inedible.

There is only one direction, holy zeal, burning with the biblical passion and desire after God in life and worship. Seek what the Father seeks. Christ has no time for cakes not turned. You must desire a faithful walk and righteous worship in true biblical reformation. Why would professing Christians *not want* God's biblically prescribed worship? I'll tell you why: they'll have small churches, with few people, and all sorts of problems arising financially for big buildings and ministries and all sorts of things people are more readily interested in rather than whether God is worshipped in the right way, or whether they walk acceptably with God in knowledge and godly fear.

People, like Ephraim, sleep, have their cake recipe ready, and when they awake, they do a little cooking (half-baked cooking) for the day of their king, and they have a party. They would much rather have a drunken party. The king will never know their cakes are not edible if he's numbed in mind.

Faithful walking and full reformation of worship must be your desire to see Christ more clearly. Desire to have as much as you can of Jesus Christ.[22] Desire to receive as much of him as you can. Desire to worship him as much as you can. Do both in spirit and truth. Unlike Ephraim, our desire should be very large to honor God as he so prescribes; we should desire a full reformation. It is only within the context of God's prescribed worship that he is found. He's found in the truth. He's not found in half-truths. Half-truths are whole lies; you've heard that. We ought, then, to burn in holy desires after God, unlike the baker sound asleep.

Psalm 27 says that the Christian's desire is one thing. "One thing I ask of the Lord," our desire after all these, is our desiring one thing in particular. We desire the grace of God, the means of grace, all the delights and comforts that Jesus Christ will give us through his Spirit to be *conformed into his image*. To desire God and to desire his benefits are the same thing. If you desire purity of worship (that which the Father seeks) and holiness of life (which Christ came to give you) then you desire God; these are all the same. Christ is found in the midst of those Spirit-motioned desires to dwell in the house of the Lord and to seek him in his temple (Psalm 27). If we have but little desires, and are contented with a little of God, we will be greatly distracted from the service of

---

[22] "But God forbid that I should glory, save in the cross of our Lord Jesus Christ, by whom the world is crucified unto me, and I unto the world," (Gal. 6:14).

God, which lies, first and foremost in glorifying him in worship. That will corrupt our holiness if we let it.

In worship we praise him for who he is and what he has done using his own word. Such a worship is immediately directed by Christ to himself, and for himself alone, that is, for his glory. He directs us in what we should do. He desires that we pick at the mind of God in the word to know what we ought not to do. In doing this, the Holy Spirit aids us in our weakness to that which God directs. Without the Holy Spirit, without Christ, we can do nothing. We cannot without his help perform what he has instructed us to do. But know, he is in nothing that he has not prescribed or directed. People believe erroneously that all they need to be is sincere and God will be in the midst of it. This is not the case, and God teaches quite the contrary to this in our text. He calls partial reformation insincere and sees such people who practice this as a cake not turned. The Holy Spirit conceives in us and motions in us the desire to live before Christ incessantly in the right way. And when we bring God's prescriptions through Christ's merit and work to him it is all acceptable; and there is nothing to slavishly fear from him.

We ought, then in all our spiritual walk and public worship in full reformation of the church, make the most excellent use we can of the good favors of God. Paul says in Romans 6:22, "But now, being made free from sin, and become servants to God, ye have your fruit unto holiness, and the end everlasting." See what he says here, you were delivered by Jesus Christ and made free from sin through God's Anointed Redeemer and Savior, made fruitful to holiness, and finally, pressed into the highway leading to everlasting life. Everlasting life is a reward, a benefit of holiness. It is a wonderful and great sign to us that God is with us when we are not distracted by the world's way of walking and the worldly way of worship that has flooded into mainstream evangelicalism, and mainstream professing reformed churches, nor should we be contented with just a little grace, or that we are insincere in our attempts at having only a partial reform in our church. We must always be those who live and worship the Father running the race of a full reformation to God's glory. For we see that partial reformation, always and of all kinds, is a full offense to God, a cake not turned.

Mark 4: Reformation and Prayer

"Surely it is meet to be said unto God, I have borne chastisement, I will not offend any more: that which I see not teach thou me: if I have done iniquity, I will do no more," (Job 34:31-32).

The Hebrew text of Job 34 is somewhat challenging. The difficulties of these verses do not necessarily expose rare or unknown words. Instead, the way these words are threaded together, and the variety of meanings that some of them allow, cause the beginning of this passage to have various meanings. We have in our translation this rendering for verse 31, "Surely it is meet to be said unto God, I have borne chastisement, I will not offend any more." In other Hebrew translations the two verses are a bit jumbled, and it is said in this way, "But to the Almighty, God who says, I forgive, I will not destroy; it ought to be said, besides what I see, teach me; if I have done iniquity, I will not offend any more." You see here, there can be a great variation on the words.

One translation I think, gives a fuller meaning to certain parts of the verse and fits the context overall. Whether the meaning revolves around chastening and affliction, or the meaning revolves around God in his omnipotent mercies to his people to forgive, the result of the exhortation is the same because the second half of the verse does *not* change.

Since this poetic work is about affliction, I tend to believe the verses make more sense around Job being *afflicted*, than at this point in some way *forgiven*, and the verses remaining set themselves parallel to one another, enforcing Elihu's exhortation.

The context of affliction seems to me to be more credible than injecting a thought of forgiveness and pardon, and having to jumble the words all around. That's important because trusting in the word of God is part of what these two verses *actually teach*. So, getting this translation right is of utmost importance.

Elihu has taken up the discourse here and is speaking to Job in verse 31, actually in all of chapter 34. Elihu has already rebuked Job's miserable comforters in chapter 32 who have missed God's righteous providence. He has already rebuked Job in chapter 33 for thinking about this affliction in an incorrect manner, as if God *owes* Job a response. Later we find Job repenting in dust and ashes for questioning God.[1] As good as Job was, he was by no means perfect. He feared God and shunned evil *and was still a sinner.*

In this 34th chapter Elihu has already covered the vast idea of God's immutable and righteous justice which he executes in all his works. No providence, affliction or method of forgiveness is unrighteous in the way God deals with sinners. If he afflicts, it is for the good of men. Whether God boasts of his mercy (as he

---

[1] "Wherefore I abhor myself, and repent in dust and ashes," (Job. 42:6).

93

does to Moses when asked to see his glory) or whether he providentially oversees all the humbling of sinners in various trials, the sinner should still respond in a specific manner. There you have the key to unlocking the translation. I do not think it should be read in this way: "I have borne chastisement, I will not offend any more," (Job. 34:31). The word *chastisement* doesn't even exist in the text. The idea of *bear something* is attached to the Hebrew idea *of committing sin.* A better translation would be: "If I have done iniquity, I will not offend any more." This is the way professing covenanters with God should respond to God. This is Elihu's point in exhorting Job to remain submitted to God's sovereignty even amidst his trial. It is considering the trial, which may be a result of sin, or it may invoke some kind of sin, and to be safe from sin Job should say, "if I have sinned, and God has brought this upon me for sin, then I will not add another sin onto sin in the way I deal with this trial." "I will not add to it," is Elihu's directive to Job to deal with God righteously.

In verse 32 there is an exhortation towards prayer and reformation, which repeats, poetically, what is said in the previous verse, which also fits well into the idea as a whole. "Teach me what I do not see; If I have done iniquity, I will do no more?" (Job. 34:32). He will not add to it, he will not do it. This is a kind of parallelism. These thoughts all complement one another.

Now Job, in his trial, has been sorely afflicted. All that is left to him is his wife, and his life. Everything else has been taken away. Possessions – all gone. Children – killed. And he is struck with boils sitting on the ash heap in an attempt to comfort himself in the physical part of his affliction. He sits on the ash heap in his affliction of boils, and later he will voluntary sprinkle himself with ashes in repentance. Now, it is a manner of comforting his pain. Later, ashes will be an emblem of his repentance. If he complains about not seeing the point of God's dealings, this would be to come against God's good providence. It is as if God is saying through Elihu to Job, "If I decide to afflict you with even those things that you deem to be so hard to bear, to such a difficult extent, am I not the God of all things who always does what is right, even in afflicting you for your good? And should you not rest contended that I am sovereign? In this, you should keep yourself from sinning against me, right?" Can Job show God where God has *erred* in this trial? Is God's hand too heavy for one who loves what is righteous and shuns what is evil? Can Job say anything other than, "teach me what I do not see." If God so desires, based on that petition, to show Job what he does to him, or rather even why, he may do so. But if God choses to simply humble his servant in affliction, causing him to submit to his sovereign will, further sanctifying Job in this trial, then this is his righteous prerogative as well.

These two verses teach three things. They teach submission. They teach prayer. They teach reformation of life. Joseph Caryl in his monumental work on Job preaches these three points separately. God has something to say about the submission of the sinner, the prayer that should accompany the submissive sinner, and the reformation of life for a submissive sinner. I'm persuaded that the verses teach *one thing*, and then shows the *manner* in which that one thing is demonstrated in two other practical duties. Elihu is saying to Job, "Submit yourself under God's hand. You are afflicted by God's ordained providence. You are bearing up yourself under the Omnipotent's trial of your resolution to serve him, and you must surrender and yield yourself to this affliction as something righteously done by God for your good. God is just in all his working. You are a mere man. In such a holy submission to God in this ordeal, you should show your submission by two practical acts of godliness, Job." So, "In your submission to God, speak this humble prayer – teach me (maybe God will answer). In your submission to God you should show forth Reformation of life in the mortification of sin before God's holy face – "I will not add to my offenses, I will do no more sin," (in other words, I will not complain or think myself ill-used)."

You see, the fruit of submission in affliction is two-fold. The submission of Job to God in dealing with "chastisement" evokes *two duties* that show the true nature of submission to God.

Submission, submitting to God, is a contented humility before Christ in full obedience of his will. This evokes two practical duties. In prayer one will petition God, "That which I do not see, teach me." In Reformation they will say, "I will not offend anymore...if I have done iniquity I will do no more." Here Job is instructed to reconsider that God is not simply the omnipotent God who providentially inflicts trials. His Holy-Spirit-lead submission not only pleases God, but will in point of effect, change him in the process by his sanctification. He is then to speak to God as Father in prayer even in affliction. God does not afflict Job simply to afflict him without reason. Affliction in this case on God's servant is to further aid Job from sinning against God no matter what providences God brings him. Does this work for Job? Does Job submit himself to God? Assuredly. "Therefore I abhor myself, And repent in dust and ashes," (Job 42:6). Such a prayer, then, in submission to God during affliction, further presses Job, or should press Job, towards reformation of life. That he does not press towards sinning, in this case, complaining, or pride, but that the desire that is cultivated is to not offend God further, and to learn from God in affliction. The desire in submission is to then sin no more. As Jesus said to the woman who was about to be stoned, "go and sin no more," (John 8:11).

We should learn from this that the fruit of submission to God is holy prayer and a reformation of life from sin. First, to understand godly submission is to understand that it is totally opposed to the world in general. Unconverted men do not like the idea of resting in a godly submission under God. They believe themselves to control their life and desire to do so. They will have nothing of yielding to Christ in all things. Oh, they may yield in things that cost them nothing, but they will not yield in all things, in the totality of the whole man and all he is. They will not demonstrate a truly penitent heart, though they might have a sorry heart once in a while. They will not lay aside their pride and stubbornness, humbly acknowledging their sins, though, sins that offend them, they will cry out against. If something comes against their person, or family, or hurts them in some way that they do not like, they will cry out against that. They will cry out at neglecting the orphans. They will start a foundation. They will give money to them. They will help them in whatever way they can. This is all good, but it is not all. They are wholly unaware that increasing their eternal happiness is done by quickened obedience to Christ's revealed will. What happens is that they do not desire submission to God's divine religion in his Law and government, by grace alone. They reject God's law and in doing so reject God's Christ. They reject God's means by which they would be made truly happy.

Submission to such things counteracts and crucifies the self-will and their desire of independence which dominates their fallen nature. That is the source of rebellion against God. They have no desire to be changed of that. In this way, they have no desire to submit their wills to God's will. Only a change made by God in the heart of such people will create true submission, which is annexed to the fruit of the Spirit in being faithful to God. God must give that new heart and must apply all of Christ's crucified benefits to the changed sinner.

Second, godly submission is yielding to God in all his ways and governance. It is to give up one's self to God in every way; that dreadful word "all". Christians do not give God lip service on Sunday and live like the devil the rest of the week. Those, we call, *hypocrites*. To give over to God, in all things, even on the ash heap, is to remain under God's hand in a submissive manner in all things. It is obedience coupled with the heart of a servant. To disavow one's self, to comply, the act of lowering, comes from the word *submittere* which is a 14th century word for a legal agreement to submit to the decision of governing arbitrators.[2] It is to yield to the government of another. Covenanted, legally bound Christian confessors, are submissive and obedient on the Lord's Day, as well as every other day, and in all circumstances. There is no sphere that the Christian lives in that is not brought into legal subjection to God's Anointed Savior. They see him as king, and they are glad to be his servants. They serve him as king in all things.

---

[2] Merriam-Webster, I. (2003). Merriam-Webster's collegiate dictionary. (Eleventh ed.). Springfield, MA: Merriam-Webster, Inc.

There are no ways of God outside the scope of godly submission.[3]

Consider the scope of Job's affliction. In light of possessions, in light of the death of his children, in the absence of health, in the midst of the worst affliction at the hand of the devil himself, even an unwise wife who said, "curse God and die," Job learns the reality of true submission to God. And he was a man who feared God and shunned evil. What is outside the scope of God's providence for him? Not a thing. Such is the case of Christians. There is no dividing line as to what God does not sovereignly reign over in the Christian's life. The Christian submits in obedience to God in all things.

Third, godly submission is the duty of every Christian. It is a submission which is clear, absolute and without exception. This is like the training of children who are to listen to their parents without question, without excuse and without delay.[4] Godly Christians act this way in light of God's revealed will for them. But it is not something that is a negative but positive action for the Christian. Submission is drawing near to God in humble service in light of his word, to seek the grace of Christ for God's glory and their good, (think through that!). Christians are the covenanted and professed subjects of the kingdom of Jesus Christ. Why would they not desire to submit themselves to the laws of his kingdom? His commandments for Christians are not

---

[3] "Submit yourselves therefore to God," (James 4:7).
[4] See Ephesians 5.

burdensome. Certainly, it is true, sometimes God must make people humble; sometimes he must use the rod instead of the staff.[5] Prideful hearts sometimes involve the long and painful process of breaking bones to fit them back in the right place.

Consider wicked Manasseh, yet later converted. God will either cause the heart to submit to him, or break the heart in affliction. But God will have his submission, and such a submissive heart will then humbly seek him. Does this not all seem rather simple, or even of such as is called common sense? But it is most difficult, is it not? Because it holds in it, the idea of submissive contentment. Considering it all joy when you face trails of many kinds to develop perseverance.

Now, coupled with submission, is the humble prayer. "Teach Me" is the humble prayer of all the godly. Elihu's exhortation is that such a prayer as this is *required.* This is the way Christians act. Strike Saul, later called Paul, and send him to the ground blinded and helpless on the road to Damascus and "behold, he prays." They are to profess their ignorance in trying to understand everything that they would like about particular providences, and sit at God's feet, Christ's feet as Mary did, to be taught.[6] Imagine all the heart-wrenching pain that could be avoided if professing Christians would simply submit themselves under God's providential direction and revealed will in

---

[5] See Psalm 23.
[6] Luke 10:42.

Scripture and pray, simply, teach me? What would the world of Christianity be like without anxiety or complaining, set in the bounds of unreserved trust in God? Take out all the complaints in the book of Job, and what does one have left in its teaching? This means that those professing Christians who have a heart of submissive stewardship before God are teachable. The Psalmist says, "You are good, and do good; Teach me Your statutes," (Psa. 119:68). God is the Christian's teacher; what a *privilege* this is. The disciples saw this in Christ, God, as their teacher. Over 50 times Christ is designated as teacher in the Gospels alone. "Nathanael answered and said to Him, "Rabbi, [teacher] You are the Son of God! You are the King of Israel!"" (John 1:49). People pay tens of thousands of dollars to be taught in elite secularized schools by teachers with limited knowledge on a variety of subjects concerning the world in some way; they go through great pains to get in, stay in, be accepted in it, get good grades and such, and pay quite a lot for the experience. Christians, by the divine illumination of the Spirit of God, have God as their teacher; and it only costs them their whole life, and all of eternity. It is one of the great promises of Christ to teach his church.[7]

This being *taught of God in humble submission* touches on two very important aspects to learning. The

---

[7] "But the Comforter, which is the Holy Ghost, whom the Father will send in my name, he shall teach you all things, and bring all things to your remembrance, whatsoever I have said unto you," (John 14:26).

source of spiritual knowledge (which is divine truth found only in Scripture and nowhere else), and the manner in which one comes to recognize this truth and knowledge (spiritual illumination – that divine and supernatural light). If Christians are submissively going to learn anything from God, to increase and progress in their sanctification, they must be taught of God, and require continual teaching from Scripture. If they are going to increase in spiritual wisdom, or further their saving knowledge of God in Christ, to abound in wisdom and prudence, they are to *learn Christ* as Christ directs, and they are to be taught by the Spirit to those ends. Christians are ignorant in so many spiritual things because they only know in part in this life. They see things dimly here on earth. Even the greatest scholars of the word see dimly. Humble Christians, though, strive to see Christ clearly through the Spirit's illumination. The Spirit is like a spotlight on Christ. He illuminates Christ in the Scriptures where there is a hearty reliance on him to understand revealed truth; the prayer is, teach me.

In opposition, ignorance is like a destructive creeping vine that wraps itself around a plant and smothers it, or like a virus that replicates itself and destroys good cells. Ignorance is not Christian, nor is it submissiveness to God. God never gives the Christian the right to be wrong about his word. His name is tied to his word, and he requires them to know that word, to both glorify him, and grow in Christ's grace themselves.

There is a great need to be constantly taught of God, refreshed in Gospel truths that one may grow in grace and the knowledge of God.[8] Such is the very prayer of the Christian submitted to the will of God. *Teach me.* And yet, they should recall and remember that every degree of grace, every point learned, everything they are taught of by God from the Bible, is a gift of grace and should be acknowledged as such.

God alone is the author of divine truth. Divine truth has its source in him. "All your children shall be taught by the LORD, and great shall be the peace of your children," (Isa. 54:13). Christ is heralded as the great exegete of the Father, declaring him, and teaching about him. "The only begotten Son, who is in the bosom of the Father, He has declared Him," (John 1:18). He is the one who reveals the spiritual depths of divine truth to the mind through the Spirit, so that the Christian's heart would be moved to further motions of righteous submissive fruit. There is a difference between proper knowledge of God and spiritual illumination of the truth. This is like reading the words on a page, in contrast to understanding the meaning behind the words. Christians can learn many things about God, but have they tasted the truth of God? They can learn truths contained in the Word; even memorize catechism questions better than others. But do they have a Spirit-filled illumination of the word for their good and

---

[8] "But grow in grace, and in the knowledge of our Lord and Savior Jesus Christ," (2 Peter 3:18).

growth?[9] Do they experience it? Do they experience Christ in it? A proper knowledge of God is nothing without the divine illumination of the Spirit of Grace making that knowledge effectual to either the saving of the soul, or the sanctification of a soul already saved. It is like the people in the Gospels who merely hear that Christ is in town, compared to the woman with the issue of blood who is touched by him and made whole personally. The difference is an infinite chasm. Here is found submission to God in holy grace, and the prayer by which the Christian seeks to be constantly taught of God, "Teach me".

If any teaching from that divine source becomes useful for the Christian, to cure the blindness of their mind, and open it to great and mighty things that "they know not", such teaching must be given by the Spirit of Truth. "It is written in the prophets, 'And they shall all be taught by God.' Therefore everyone who has heard and learned from the Father comes to Me," (John 6:45). "But you have an anointing from the Holy One, and you know all things," (1 John 2:20). Through Christ, through the Spirit sent of Christ, the Christian learns from Christ, from the word, by the power of the Spirit. Consider, then, what kind of privilege is it to be taught by God himself? Thomas Manton said of such people, "It is a blessed privilege to be taught of God, to be made wise to salvation, and not only to get an ear to hear, but

---

[9] "But call to remembrance the former days, in which, after ye were illuminated, ye endured a great fight of afflictions," (Heb. 10:32).

a heart to understand, and learn by hearing, not only the power to believe, but the very act of faith itself."[10] Think about it – taught *of Christ himself.*

What is this knowledge that causes Job-like submission to affliction to the point of humble prayer to "teach me?" It is the grand mystery of godliness and redemption that flows from the covenantal heart of the Triune God fulfilled in Christ. "Because it has been given to you to know the mysteries of the kingdom of heaven," (Matt. 13:11). And know that Christ said about others, "to them it has not been given." There is privilege in divine illumination. Some have this, and some do not. Some grow in grace, and others not. To some the kingdom is given, and to others, not. People may certainly have the Bible in their hand and still have blinders on their eyes. Such a knowledge is not saving, nor transforming in the eternal sense, for those people. Such a blindness in spiritual things shows emphatically, that they do not have the Spirit, and they are not spiritually minded. Such people as Lamentations says, "wandered blind in the streets," (Lam. 4:14). They may be able to tell others all about the substance of the Bible, but without the contrite and humble submissive heart that God grants through the Spirit, they have no light in them. The mysteries of godliness are not transforming unless they are seen in their own light, in the divine light of the law and the Gospel empowered through the

---

[10] Manton, Thomas, *The Complete Works of Thomas Manton*, Volume 9, (Worthington, IL: Maranatha Publications, 1979) 249.

glasses of the Spirit of God, to see Christ clearly. "In Your light we see light," (Psa. 36:9).

All true and genuine children of the Most High God have God's personal teaching.[11] In all this supernatural, Spirit-illuminated understanding, they have the Father and the Son, to teach them by the Spirit. Again, Christ speaks of himself, "they shall be all taught of God; he therefore that heard and learned of my Father, comes to me." And, "the Spirit, when he is come, he shall lead you into all truth." He says, "My sheep hear my voice." Knowing that they must pray this prayer, "teach me" argues that there is an ignorance; and any ignorance found by a submissive Christian makes them more serious with God to be taught of him to escape that ignorance. They beg God for constant direction and fresh impartations of the Spirit of illumination. Would it not be very dangerous to be left to one's own self without the Spirit teaching them?

Elihu's second exhortation after "teach me" was to "offend God no more" or to have a *Reformation of Life*. "If I have done iniquity, I will do no more." This is reform: biblical reformation. Such reformation of life is a submissive, prayerful dealing with sin. A godly person who recognizes sin as sin, will not avoid only a single sin, but all sin. There are myriads of groups here and there through the last hundred years of church history that climb on some political bandwagon to fight against one

---

[11] "But ye have an unction from the Holy One, and ye know all things," (1 John 2:20).

particular sin at the expense of being narrow-minded towards Scripture's teaching about all sin. Certainly, there are sins in our country that require Christians to take stands on specific occasions. There is no doubt to that. But the Word of God never says, just focus on one sin at the expense of the rest.[12] Sanctifying power does not work in that way. It never says, once I get over this sin, I will work on another, later. This implies that a soul remains in sin, willfully before it overcomes whatever sin it is dealing with at the time. Instead, the submissive, prayerful Christian cries over and over to defeat remaining sin which tries to rear its ugly head in so many ways. It will especially raise its ugly head in the midst of trials and difficulties as it did with Job. The devil said, "But now, stretch out Your hand and touch all that he has, and he will surely curse You to Your face" (Job. 1:11). What *is* complaining? What *is* pride, or even religious confusion to God's providence? Such sin sounds different said that way. They are far less intense. But is it not a cursing of God in some way? Did Job sin against God? Was the devil right in his assessment of Job? Is it simple speech, or is it just a different manner of sin? Is sin not cursing God to his face? "In all this did not Job sin *with his lips,*" (Job. 2:10). But this is chapter 2, what of chapter 34? Or 42? Job sinned in believing that the Lord owed him a full answer to the reason for his suffering. God speaks to him, and reveals that Job as a

---

[12] "For if ye live after the flesh, ye shall die: but if ye through the Spirit do mortify the deeds of the body, ye shall live," (Rom. 8:13).

creature had no right to question God, or his wisdom, (chapters 38-41). Job repented of his sin in 42:1-6. Sin is to violate God's Law, or, to leave off from God's Law what he requires. You will hear many today say, "No Law, only grace." "I believe in Jesus! And that's enough for me!" The demons believe things too and that doesn't argue *their* salvation. Such a warped and sinful way of looking at the Gospel is not illuminated by the Holy Spirit. That is the carnal man speaking. It is one who does not want to be told what to do, nor does he want to leave off his sins, but rather finds a cloak for them, and to have some form of religion too.[13] Jesus said it this way, "Why do you call Me 'Lord, Lord,' and do not do the things which I say? *[What does He say?]* "Whoever comes to Me, and hears My sayings and does them, I will show you whom he is like: "He is like a man building a house, who dug deep and laid the foundation on the rock. And when the flood arose, the stream beat vehemently against that house, and could not shake it, for it was founded on the rock. "But he who heard and did nothing is like a man who built a house on the earth without a foundation, against which the stream beat vehemently; and immediately it fell. And the ruin of that house was great," (Luke 6:46-49). Whose sayings? God's sayings. Where are those found? Through the divine Word, when Jesus spoke this, all of it is found in the Old Testament. And there is much effort in building a house.

---

[13] "and they declare their sin as Sodom, they hide it not. Woe unto their soul! for they have rewarded evil unto themselves," (Isa. 3:9).

It is not something that just appears all of a sudden. The Old Testament requires much work to understand rightly. Is it not a blessing that we have the New Testament to understand the Old Testament?

To know the Word of God is to know God's mind for life and godliness, for faith and practice.[14] Submission prompts the sinner to live in the constant state of killing sin, and becoming more holy. They find these instructions in the divine Word of God, illuminated to them by the Holy Spirit when they pray "teach me" so that they will not offend God again. They long to be taught so that they learn to sin no more. They know how to deal with the devil, for we are not unaware of his devices. They know how to be spiritually enabled to defeat sin, by walking in the light of truth. They know how to deal with remaining sin, to put on Christ and walk in the Spirit. Is this all in an instant, or are they required by God to pray teach me? Is this not something all through the Christian walk? This is why it is called a walk.[15] Such professing Christians are very suspicious of themselves because they know, truly, in submission to God, what it means to be contrite and poor in spirit; how to be submissive. They know, with Job, they are really worms. "How much less man, who is a maggot, ... who is a worm?" (Job 25:6). Reformation in this sense is very

---

[14] "And that from a child thou hast known the holy scriptures, which are able to make thee wise unto salvation through faith which is in Christ Jesus," (2 Tim. 3:15).
[15] "That ye would walk worthy of God, who hath called you unto his kingdom and glory," (1 Thess. 2:12).

difficult throughout the Christian life. People often do not like to think of themselves in such a debased way. But this is because they often have a low view of God and high view of man. But the submissive Christian considers, "If I have done iniquity..." if sin is found in me through examination, it will be rectified and I will add no more to it; I will reform. David prayed that he would be cleansed from both presumptuous sins and secret faults. Cleanse me from things I don't even know I have done, which is part of Elihu's exhortation to Job.

The Christian looking to please Christ always has a suspected heart, and reformation uses that as fuel to mortify sin and grow in holiness. He is constantly placing himself in the police lineup looking for what he may have done outside or in violation of God's will. This becomes tedious to him only because he longs for the day in which he will sin against Christ's blood no more. But he does know he has God, and that he has God through Christ. How does one "offend God no more?" How does one reform in this context? The Hebrew there in verse 31 really says "add to it," as if sin is there and no more sin will be added to it. The remedy to this is very simple: cast off that which is opposed to Christ, and then put on Christ bringing Christ to every duty. When the Christian acts in submissive faith to Christ as Mediator to any duty, that is the most important ingredient in acceptance of that duty to God.

Christ is the altar by which every spiritual sacrifice is to be offered. It does not matter how great men might seem to be in church, in the way they act or serve, for anything done in duty before God in their natural strength or power is not accepted unless it is offered up through Jesus. Every submissive act must rest by faith on Jesus when it is given or accomplished for God, otherwise, God rejects it. Concerning worship, Jeremiah Burroughs said, "How many men and women have been professors of religion twenty or thirty years, and yet are not acquainted with this great mystery of godliness, to tender up everything in worship to God in the name of his Son? ... because it is a principal part of the great mystery of the Gospel. Without this, all our duties are rejected of God, and cast away."[16] There is no ability not to offend God without the Mediator Jesus Christ. Men without Christ not only don't please God in anything they do, but everything they do counts against them for not doing it in submissive obedience, prayer and reformation of life in Christ's power. "So then, those who are in the flesh cannot please God," (Rom. 8:8).

This was Elihu's exhortation to afflicted Job, that the fruit of submission to God is holy prayer and reformation of life. So, are *you* submissive to God in all things? What does submission look like in your life? How would you describe it to another? Christ was submissive and he was God. "Though he were a Son, yet learned he obedience by the things which he suffered; And being made perfect, he became the author of eternal

---

[16] Burroughs, Jeremiah, *Gospel Worship*, (Crossville, TN: Puritan Publications, 2018) 147.

salvation unto all them that obey him," (Heb. 5:8-9). All things fulfilled by him, wielding the power of the Spirit without measure, reconciling his people through the cross, satisfying divine justice, exalted to the right hand of God, to interceded for you in order to give you his Spirit to lead you in a life of submission. What does submission look like in light of affliction? For most Christians, affliction is a main vein running through most of their life. Are you stoic? Do you simply press through hard times? What do you constantly rest on? There must be in you a continual desire and motivation to prove out your prayer and your reformation. You must be resolved to carry your Christian demeanor solely by Christ's grace, and we carry on in this grace when we constantly pursue a holy submission to his will. This is a daily, habitual, constant submission. It's never manic. It's not up and down, now and then, sometimes or other. You know that you carry in your heart the remaining influences of sin, though the old man is dead. That opposition is always in your heart. You need a happy, unwavering and continuous obedience to Christ in submission to his will.

You should have this happy demeanor to do God's will in every duty you render to him. Those duties might not be perfect, and you know it; but God accepts from his people their willingness in the duty. He will never, at any time, or for any reason, accept the duty without heart-work. Christ does not look merely for service from you, but looks for delightful service from you. A willful joyful submission to be taught and to reform. This is where you love him in sincerity. He says, 1 John 5:3, "This is love, to keep his commandments, and his commandments are not burdensome." Working for Christ is never grievous to you, but it must be pleasant. Cain offered sacrifice with Abel in Genesis 4, but he did it as a begrudging work. But if your heart is set in submission to God in truth and holiness, you are never forced in service to him.

Rather, religious service to Christ in this way is natural, genuine and sincere. It should be an unwavering obedience in you. I know you find this hard. To be unwavering is very hard. But that is the ideal. You may have embarked on this journey thinking the Christian life is a bed of roses, and come to find out it's harder to be a Christian that not. You have come to serve God for your whole life. You are hoping that you end the race in an unwavering submission to God's will as you began it. Many falter at this, not ending as well as they began. You look for a constant spring of holiness in your life, and you hope that with all your might, you bring acceptable sacrifices to God. Yet, you know, without Christ, you can do nothing. You have to bring Christ to everything. God desires that you have a sincere, and unwavering "heart to serve him," (Deut. 5:29).

Happy, unwavering and further, you are to be *constant*. Judas was a disciple for a *time* wasn't he? We find that he has a heart-problem. "Satan entered into his heart," (Luke 22:3). You find that in lost people, their hearts are not filled with the Spirit, and they are filled with the devil. But when Jesus and the Father dwell with the Christian, they send the Spirit to dwell in a special manner. To constantly produce in them the fruits of righteousness, little by little, here a little, there a little. God dwells there and that is what makes you constant in fruitfulness.

If you don't have a happy, unwavering and constant heart of submission to God, there is no way that you will pray "teach me" nor will you ever say "I will not add to my offenses." Without that sincere submissive heart, all you do in religion will be in vain. All the hard duties you do will be undone, and it will make you hate the religious life; it will exasperate you. If grace is not in your heart cultivating a love to the Lord Jesus Christ in sincerity, everything Christ asks of you will never come to pass in the way God requires. God's first gift of grace in Christ is a new heart: Ezek. 36:26, "A new heart also will I give unto you, and a new spirit will I put within you." Without a new heart what can you do? Nothing pleasing to God. You are at enmity with Him.

If you do have this new heart, and you have this desire for a happy, unwavering and constant submission to God in all his providences in your life, you are inclined to do His will. Yes, you will fail; you will sin; you will try to manufacture something you want or need. Paul said in Romans 7:18, "To will is present with me, yet how to perform that which is good I find not." The duties you engage in to be taught by God and used to reform your life, but they always come short of God's perfect ideal in your efforts. And you cannot treat God as a genie in this. You cannot wish it into reality hoping he'll grant it all at once. You look to do duty with a sincere and loving heart, but you do it poorly. You get mere tastes of grace, which in turn press you find just a bit more.

Consider your prayers and your reformation in this. Do your prayers originate from a submissive heart? Prayer itself is submissive in that it seeks help from outside itself, to One greater than itself. It is true that people pray to all kinds of idols. Are they praying submissively to God when they pray to Buddha? Or Allah? Or an idol like Brahman? No.

The act of prayer, though a position of submission, may not be submissive in any way; they simply want what they want and will pray to whomever to get it, even if it's just to make them feel better. True prayer must be born of a submissive heart, a repentant heart that serves the Anointed Savior. Heart-work is first. It is *always* first. Submission comes second, a yielding to God and his revealed will in humility. Prayer comes third.

Also make a note on this, it's a dangerous thing to pray as Elihu instructed. *Teach me* is opening a box that you might not like. God *answers* those prayers. He will teach you. You must be spiritually ready for prayers like that. Teach me...contentment. Teach me...to love that which is unlovely in my enemies. Teach me...to learn contentedness. Teach me...to sin no more. Teach me what I do not know. Those are very spiritual prayers, but they open up a rain from heaven that will seem sometimes like a flood in your life. Be ready to pray those; be ready to pray in that way. Are all your resolutions and reformations from a submissive heart, proceeding out of a submissive prayer? It is dangerous to be left in any part of our duty to ourselves. Duty in your own hands is a terrible thought to Christians. Imagine if God said to you as he said to the church of old, "Ephraim is joined to idols, let him alone." Scary! Doing things in our own strength, not relying on the Spirit of God having tasted that the Lord is good is a scary proposition. We ought to have no desire to work any work without Christ's help. He's the one who sends the Spirit to produce fruit in us. Sin is involved in your difficult afflicted life as a Christian. Not until glory will you escape it. It is, though, all about how you handle it, as Elihu exhorted Job.

Submissive in your disposition to God, you pray to him, boldly coming to Christ for grace, the ascended Son of Man and high Priest, and then you resolve to walk as becoming a Christian, every day, all the time as your Lord instructs. When you sin, you are mindful not to add a further sin to this. Your desire is to break it off, and behead it with the sword of the Spirit. Can you die for Christ in holy submission, so to speak, as Christ died for you to do the Father's will that you would be saved? You are not only instructed by Christ to follow him, but also, Jesus says that unless you bear his cross, you can have no part in him.[17] Henry Smith said, "Therefore, we are called servants to show how we should obey; we are called soldiers to show how we should suffer," (Luke 12:38; 2 Tim. 2:3).[18] Whether or not you decided to pray and reform this very minute, if you resolve never to add a single point to sin again, regardless of your sincerity and resolve, you are already obliged by Christ's command never to sin: he's told you to go and sin no more. Such a religious reformation of life is part of what it means to enter into covenant with God. God's right over your yielding to him, or your submissiveness to him, whether you pray to him teach me or not, or whether you offend him or not, is valid whether you will consent to do it or not; or even how well you do it. But it is far sweeter to obey Christ and taste the kisses of his mouth which is much more sweeter than wine, as the bride who yields to her husband in all things, than to rebel against him.

To live a life of sin is to live like a wicked man in rebellion against God. The proud and arrogant are hell-bound. Consider the terror of all proud and arrogant men. They might look to get rid of some sins, sins they don't like. They may even go through all kinds of pains to get rid of certain sin because it is causing them some distress. Distress to their health. Distress at work. Distress in their family. They are looking for temporal

---

[17] "Then said Jesus unto his disciples, if any man will come after me, let him deny himself, and take up his cross, and follow me," (Matt. 16:24).

[18] Smith, Henry, *A Treatise on the Lord's Supper*, (Coconut Creek, FL: Puritan Publications, 2013) 93.

relief. But, it is never about just 12 steps to take care of one sin. "Everyone proud in heart is an abomination to the LORD; Though they join forces, none will go unpunished," (Prov. 16:5). "Pride goes before destruction," (Prov. 16:18). The Apostle James tells us that God *resists the proud.*[19] Verses like these ought to frighten their sleepy consciences, unless for whatever reason, they want the Lord to abhor them, to curse them, to fight against them, and utterly to destroy them. Instead, they should run to Christ, who alone is able to heal them of the corruption of their sinful natures, that they might learn to be humble in Christ's school to pray and live before him in holy submission. If they don't do this, it will be a very unhappy and crying end to their life, and terror beginning in eternity in hell forever. God will manifest his displeasure against them, as he did against Pharaoh, Herod, and other such prideful people. So, take this to heart, and be taught by Elihu. The fruit of submission to God is the holy prayer "teach me" and a reformation of life from sin is the resolution that "I will no longer offend." In these, all Christians are resolved.

---

[19] "But he giveth more grace. Wherefore he saith, God resisteth the proud, but giveth grace unto the humble," (James 4:6).

Mark 5: The Spirit in Biblical Reformation

"So then they that are in the flesh cannot please God," (Rom. 8:8). And, "For as many as are led by the Spirit of God, they are the sons of God," (Rom. 8:14).

Look first to the context of Romans 8. We find Paul's letter to the Romans is *very* theological in nature, with an abundance of practical outworking. Jumping into the middle of this work may be for some confusing based on an unfamiliarity with the letter as a whole. It is a meticulous theological exposition on the Gospel's relation to the Law of God, and to the righteousness of God as it is applied to both individuals in the kingdom of God and to the church as a whole; and it centers on the free grace of Christ, and the life of the Christian led by the Spirit sent of Christ.

It was most likely written by Paul from Corinth, the capital of Achaia, after his second journey for the purpose of collecting the financial aid needed for the church at Jerusalem. In the 15th chapter he says that he was going to Jerusalem to minister to the saints. "For," he adds, "it hath pleased them of Macedonia and Achaia to make a certain contribution for the poor saints which are at Jerusalem." It was written prior to Paul going to Rome. This is important because it was written before his final letters of Ephesians and Philippians, Hebrews (most likely) and Philemon, and Second Timothy. It is generally received as written around the time of the year AD 57. This would have been about twenty–four years after the ascension of the Lord.

The verses in question are set in the midst of chapter 8; here is an overview of the letter up to that point.

In 1:1–16 we find a salutation, and an introduction.

In 1:17–11:36 we find the exposition of Paul's understanding of the doctrine of the righteousness of God, proposed, established, and expounded; 8:8 and 14 are set in this section.

All mankind is liable to the wrath of God. Ch. 1:18–2:29.

The heathen world in general. Ch. 1:18–32.

Those also who judge others, including the Jews. Ch. 2:1–29.

Certain objections are given with regard to the Jews. Ch. 3:1–8.

The testimony of the Old Testament to universal sinfulness is given. Ch. 3:9–20.

The righteousness of God, manifested in Christ, and apprehended by faith, set forth as the sole remedy, available for those who believe. Ch. 3:21–31.

Abraham is shown to have been justified by faith, and not by works, and so, covenanted Christian disciples exercising true regenerate faith being his true heirs. Ch. 4:1–25.

Results of the revelation of the righteousness of God. Ch. 5:1–21.

The blessings of righteousness (5:1–11).

The imputation of righteousness (5:12–21).

There are moral conclusions made about believers after this. Ch. 6:1–8:39.

There is the obligation to holiness of life from them. Ch. 6:1–7:6.

How the Law of God prepares the soul for freedom in Christ and from the dominion of sin. Ch. 7:7–25.

Then there is chapter 8 where is found the blessed condition and assurance of hope of those that are in Christ, and walk after the Spirit. Ch. 8:1–39.

The righteousness of Christ in salvation, election, and God's sovereign decree.

And we arrive at Romans 8:8 and 14. "So then, those who are in the flesh cannot please God." (Rom. 8:8). "For as many as are led by the Spirit of God, these are sons of God." (Rom. 8:14).

Concerning verse 8, unregenerate men, those lost, those not born from above, live in a state of sin and misery. They are unknowingly plagued not only with original sin credited to their account by Adam, as a result of Adam's failed test in the garden, but they are unknowingly plagued by actual sins which come out of original sin. This involves this sin nature, and the sins that come out of their sin nature. This pertains to what they are, and what they do. Original sin makes them what they are: fallen. Actual sins show what they do: sin. In both they are blinded and dead in sin. All mankind is involved by nature, through the fall of Adam, the common root of all mankind (Rom. 5:12, with Gen. 3), in this state of sin and misery, as the 1647 Westminster Confession states.[1] All mankind is, by nature, at their very conception, dead in sins and trespasses, and children of wrath (Eph. 2:1-3), haters of God until their conversion. This is why those who are in the flesh, cannot possibly please God, (Romans 8:8). God considers them dead corpses unable to uphold one single point of obedience well, much less perfectly, which is the Law's standard.

Living according to this fleshly state is living in opposition to being led by the Spirit. Such people in the flesh, do not have the power to please God. It's because dead people have no power. Literally, Paul says "those who are in the flesh have no power to please God." The word "cannot" is rather weak in comparison to the more literal phrase "having no power." Depravity is often described to inquirers on the topic that carnal men have no power to do good in their wicked state; not just that they cannot. Paul's description, this biblical description, is that they have *no power.* Concerning verse 14, those Christians the Lord Christ has saved from both the condemnation of original sin and the further aggravation

---

[1] *1647 Westminster Confession of Faith* 6:4. See also, *1647 Westminster Shorter Catechism* question 17.

of all their actual sins, are led by the Spirit of God. What a wonderful statement this is. People redeemed by Jesus, by free grace, and under all the benefits of Christ's work, through the Spirit live to Christ, and are not dead. These are people who have been made alive, and are led by the Spirit. In spiritual things Christians are like little children who are led by the hand of their father; they are not childish, but they are child-like, led by the Spirit hand in hand. In this instance, the Spirit of God leads them by the hand to be guided. He does not lead them kicking and screaming. He leads them by sanctifying their wills that they would conform to the pattern and image of the Son of God. This occurs as they imitate Christ, and so are conformed to his nature, and the Spirit changes their very desires and wills to be led by him. The Spirit's spiritual and mysterious influence changes the person's wicked resistance to holiness into holy agreement.

The leading of the Spirit not only involves leading his people into holiness by conforming them to Christ, but also by enlightening their understandings to know what is happening to them, and what will happen to them. Christ says, "When He the Spirit of truth is come, He will guide you into all truth." All Christians who are led by the Spirit of God are led into truth consistent with the Scriptures and the will of God; however much or little this might be; 30, 60, or 100 fold.[2]

---

[2] Mark 4:8.

Later, the Apostle Paul will tell the reader that they are to be transformed by the constant renewing of their mind in Romans 12. All Christians are led by the Spirit to this kind of spiritual transformation, this continual renewing. Or, it may be said, they are led by the Spirit to be motioned toward godly Reformation. When the Christian has their heart changed and mind enlightened, being led by the Spirit, they are able, as the Apostle explains, to prove that which is the good, acceptable, and perfect will of God.

All the mysteries of godliness are opened up for these Christians. Christ is opened up to them. The fountain of grace is accessible to them. Rivers of living water flow from them.[3] This does not mean that the Holy Spirit leads by way of perfection in every duty these Christians engage in. The way of salvation is always perfect; all the means of grace are perfect ways toward further conforming to Christ. The duties Christians are to engage in are given in perfect ideals. Do not lie. Do not lust. Do not love the world. Worship God in spirit and truth. Love God, love Christ, love your neighbor, love your enemies, and the like. But because of remaining sin the duties themselves are not perfected in their exercise. The Apostle James says in his letter that "in many things we all offend," (James 3:2). And just previous to chapter 8 of Romans, Paul writes, "What I want to do I do not do and that which I hate, this I keep on doing." What this being led by the Spirit indicates is

---

[3] John 7:38.

that all those guided by the hand of the Spirit in this way, walk in a contrary direction to those who walk in the flesh. It may be that certain enticements cause the Christian to lust for something of the world, and they fall into sin, and wobble instead of walk, and this happens daily, but yet, there is a Spirit-fashioned principle at work in them which resists and contends against that fleshly lifestyle. Such a Spirit led walk engages in putting to death the deeds of the body, instead of offending God to add sin to sin. And in the last chapter we saw the penitent one in Job praying that he would be taught, and that he would not add sin to sin. This is the ideal. The deeds of the body are mortified (killed) by the leading of the Spirit, but they are mortified slowly, and that, day by day.

This Holy Spirit leads those in whom he dwells so that remaining sin will be killed; and they will be set apart for service to Christ. The Spirit's job is to take the glory and work of the person of Jesus, God manifested in the flesh, and the benefits of his offices (Prophet, Priest and King), the one Mediator, and shine the light of truth to discern the work and power of the Anointed Savior. He shows them that they were once entangled in bondage, unable to please God by the righteous standard of the law. He shows that all are condemned according to this law. He then convinces these people of sin. He shows them the gracious way of escape which is through free grace in Christ. He shows them their need of the mercy of God in Christ's imputed righteousness to them, and leads them to cast away everything they may do or think or walk in their own strength. Instead, they look to Jesus Christ and acceptance to God through the Savior's work. He shows them there is nothing they can do of their own accord to find any degree of acceptability before God as a sinner. And he shows them they need the Savior at every step, all of free unmerited favor from God.

This indwelling Spirit teaches them, as the Spirit of truth who enlightens the Christian mind, to understand Christ's gift of salvation through the holy word of God. The Spirit points to Christ, exalts Christ, magnifies Christ, and shows the new convert that by grace alone, through faith in Christ alone, they may be guided, and brought to the Lord Jesus for all their needs. All spiritual benefits that reside in Christ are granted to such believers through the Spirit of Grace who leads them. The Spirit leads to Christ through the truth of the Word. "Teach me to do Your will, For You are my God; Your Spirit is good. Lead me in the land of uprightness. Revive me, O LORD, for Your name's sake! For Your righteousness' sake bring my soul out of trouble," (Psa. 143:10-11).

Such Spirit led Christians who trust in the Lord Jesus, who have been renewed in their mind, and transformed to engage in the mortification of sin, are called sons of God. In Scripture there are a two uses to the term "sons of God." One is of Jesus, and one is the elect, or the worshipping saint. By nature, the title belongs to Jesus Christ alone. Jesus alone is the divine Son of God - the only-begotten Son of God.[4] But it is by grace these Christians are also called sons of God. "That the sons of God saw the daughters of men that they were fair; and they took them wives of all which they chose," (Gen. 6:2). The sons of God being the line of the woman against the seed of the serpent. "Now there was a day when the sons of God came to present themselves before the LORD, and Satan came also among them," (Job. 1:6). During a worship service where the sons of God present themselves before the Lord in church. "When the morning stars sang together, and all the sons of God shouted for joy?" (Job 38:7), where angels and men praised God for all the good of creation. Such men have been born again by grace through the Spirit. The New Testament is filled with these instances. "But as many as received him, to them gave he power to become the sons of God, even to them that believe on his name," (John 1:12). This is the grace found in redemption through Christ, where Christians are called the sons of God.[5]

Christians are made sons and daughters of God through adoption. All those that are justified God promises, in and for his only Son Jesus Christ, to make

---

[4] " And lo a voice from heaven, saying, this is my beloved Son, in whom I am well pleased," (Matt. 3:17).

[5] "Behold, what manner of love the Father hath bestowed upon us, that we should be called the sons of God: therefore the world knoweth us not, because it knew him not. Beloved, now are we the sons of God, and it doth not yet appear what we shall be: but we know that, when he shall appear, we shall be like him; for we shall see him as he is," (1 John 3:1-2).

partakers of the grace of adoption. In this Christians are taken into the number, and enjoy the liberties and privileges of the children of God. They have his name put upon them. They receive the Spirit of adoption themselves. They have access to the throne of grace with boldness to present themselves before him as acceptable sacrifices in worship. They are enabled to cry, *Abba, Father.* They are pitied, protected, provided for. They are sealed to the day of redemption, and inherit the promises, as heirs of everlasting salvation.[6] Christ adopts wicked people changed and led by the Spirit of free grace. These people are led by the Spirit, by the hand, back to Jesus Christ to keep his words and follow his ways.

In these verses, Paul gives various proofs to being a child of God; a son or daughter. This first proof, verse 14, is being led by the Spirit of God. This is a proof of salvation. The title, sons of God, should cause the Christian a great amount of hope and comfort, because they are not like those who walk in the flesh, who have no power to please God. Instead, they have been led by the Spirit to serve God in such a capacity as to be able (a word of power) to please him. And all they do, to please him, is imperfect. But in Christ, God receives it all as perfect because he receives it as Christ has done it.

So, these two verses show forth two kinds of people. One kind is in the flesh, who are not led by the

---

[6] "And grieve not the holy Spirit of God, whereby ye are sealed unto the day of redemption," (Eph. 4:30).

Spirit. They are captive to original sin, only sin, and have no power, in any capacity, to please God in any point of religion. They are God haters and rebels. The second kind have been changed, given a new heart, walk with the Spirit, are led by the Spirit by the hand to Christ, in order to render service to Christ as obedient sons and daughters. With this in mind, hear the doctrine to be taken from these two verses.

Reformation of life is impossible without the Spirit of God. Mankind is made up of two parts primarily. The material (body). The immaterial (soul). "And fear not them which kill the body, but are not able to kill the soul," (Matthew 10:28). The covenant of Adam in the garden rendered this material and immaterial being cursed and fallen by God's appointment. Both the body and soul are corrupted as a result of the curse of God on the fall of man. This does not mean that people act out being as a bad as they can be in actual sins, but rather, that the effects of the fall have completely and totally ruined the entire being of man. It is not just that man's mind is ruined, or that just his body is ruined, or that just his soul ruined. The whole man is corrupted with original sin. Original sin corrupts them to be as utterly fallen in Adam as they can be. They can be no more fallen in Adam than they are. As a result of this fall, where the narrative is found in Genesis 3, mankind cannot fundamentally do anything to please God. *Any thing. No-thing.* He is kicked out of the garden, and the way to paradise is barred. Original sin renders them incompetent in every way. It renders them, as Paul explains in Romans 8 and Ephesians 2, without any power to please God, dead in sin. It makes them stupid to believe that running away from the sin, and covering themselves with a fig leaf is better than repentance. Isaiah 64:6 states, "But we are all as an unclean thing, and all our righteousness are as filthy rags; and we all do fade as a leaf; and our iniquities, like the wind, have taken us away." Even actions that people think are good and righteous in the eyes of God, are in fact filthy rags because of this original sin in them. The "filthy rag" is a designation of a used menstruating cloth of a woman's period. Any *thing* men do that may seem good, their best good, their best righteousness, their best works, their best intentions, their best desires, are at best, filthy rags; and this was written to the people of God.

In Genesis 6:5, shortly after the fall, "God saw that the wickedness of man was great in the earth, and that every imagination of the thoughts of his heart was only evil continually." The abundance of Scriptural references to the depravity of man in this way is quite plain. As a result of the fall, man is only evil and every thought is evil. Those who deny this show forth their evilness. This evil disposition begins at conception. It does not begin when acts of the will are committed that do not reach God's standard. There is no age of accountability. Men are not sinners because they sin, rather, they sin because they are sinners. Psalm 51:5 is exceedingly clear, "Behold, I was shapen in iniquity; and in sin did my mother conceive me." Even at the moment of conception, David said that he was "conceived a sinner." This evil heart, birthed at conception, is so completely extensive that man cannot will to do any good even from that time forth. From conception they *will* only evil before God.

The will of man is bound to evil and it is only engaged in self-love and hatred to God. In this, as Paul previously explained in Romans chapter 1 and chapter 3, men suppress truth, suppress God, and exalt themselves. This is a God-hater. Consider, then, these 4 main points to this biblical truth of original and actual sin.

[1] Fallen man cannot do or work any good. Matthew 7:17-18, "Even so every good tree bringeth forth good fruit; but a corrupt tree bringeth forth evil fruit. A good tree cannot bring forth evil fruit, neither can a corrupt tree bring forth good fruit." 1 Cor. 12:3, "Wherefore I give you to understand, that no man speaking by the Spirit of God calleth Jesus accursed: and that no man can say that Jesus is the Lord, but by the Holy Ghost." Cannot do it, cannot work it.

[2] Fallen man cannot understand in full or understand in part that which is good. Ephesians 4:18, "Having their understanding darkened, being alienated from the life of God through the ignorance that is in them, because of the blindness of their heart." John 8:43, "Why do ye not understand my speech? even because ye cannot hear my word." Matthew 13:14, "And in them is

fulfilled the prophecy of Esaias, which saith, By hearing ye shall hear, and shall not understand; and seeing ye shall see, and shall not perceive." 1 Cor. 2:14; "But the natural man receiveth not the things of the Spirit of God: for they are foolishness unto him: neither can he know them, because they are spiritually discerned."

[3] Fallen man cannot have any desire towards that which is good. Matthew 7:18, "A good tree cannot bring forth evil fruit, neither can a corrupt tree bring forth good fruit." John 3:3, "Jesus answered and said unto him, Verily, verily, I say unto thee, Except a man be born again, he cannot see the kingdom of God." Ephesians 2:1, 5, "And you hath he quickened, who were dead in trespasses and sins; Even when we were dead in sins, hath quickened us together with Christ, (by grace ye are saved)."

[4] Fallen man is wholly opposed to any good in every way. This does not mean they act as bad as they could act in actual sins. It simply means they are affected in every area of their being totally, and wholly opposed to the good things of God. Genesis 6:5, "And God saw that the wickedness of man was great in the earth, and that every imagination of the thoughts of his heart was only evil continually." Jeremiah 13:23, "Can the Ethiopian change his skin, or the leopard his spots? then may ye also do good, that are accustomed to do evil." Jeremiah 17:9, "The heart is deceitful above all things, and desperately wicked: who can know it?"

As a result, these 4 points show that this original sin cripples men being incapable of doing any good in the eyes of God. William Ames said, "Bondage to sin consists in man's being so captivated by sin that he has no power to rise out of it...rather he would wallow in it."[7] *The Synod of Dort* took great pains to study and determine the truth of this. They studied the viability of what is called Arminian Doctrine. Arminianism teaches that men are affected by the fall, but not completely fallen. They also have the free exercise of their will to do good. This was wholly opposed to Scripture and condemned as heretical by the church. Dordt said, "...all men are conceived in sin, and are by nature children of wrath, incapable of saving good, prone to evil, dead in sin, and in bondage thereto; and without the regenerating grace of the Holy Spirit, they are neither able nor willing to return to God, to reform the depravity of their nature, or to dispose themselves to reformation."

People like to think they are good; people like to think others are good, good natured, good people, good generally speaking. They like to think they have power to please God in doing good things. The Bible, in opposition to that, teaches that man, apart from free grace in Christ, is spiritually dead and cannot please God. A dead man feels nothing. It does not matter what is done to him. Kick him, punch him, cut off his arm with a sword, he does not feel anything; why? He's dead. So, a

---

[7] Ames, William, *The Marrow of Theology*, (Grand Rapids, MI: Baker Books, 1997) 57.

man who is spiritually dead does not feel the weight of his sins, or his need of Jesus Christ who redeems from sin. Though his sins might be a heavy burden weighing him down into the pit of hell, still, he feels...nothing. He is a stranger to the mystery of godliness, past feeling, given over to a reprobate sense, so that he does not feel the weight and burden of all his sins. "The soul that sins [in that way] shall die," (Ezekiel 18:20).

Anything God says to someone in the flesh, someone still in their original sin, still in bondage to sin, still under the power of evil, and the power of the devil, anything they hear, try or do as it relates to God's Law and requirements for holiness is a right command and directive, but to the sinner, it is useless because they cannot do it. They have no ability to hear much less do what God says, as much as a rock or stone might have some ability to do spiritual things in and of itself. In this, consider, reformation of life is impossible without the Spirit of God. Reformation of life is only possible *through* the Spirit of God.

Such a gracious salvation and indwelling of the Spirit (walking in Him) is true of a Christian in any age of the church. For Paul says in Romans 8:9, one verse after 8, "But you are not in the flesh but in the Spirit, if indeed the Spirit of God dwells in you. Now if anyone does not have the Spirit of Christ, he is not His." If one does not "have" the Spirit, meaning to have, *i.e.* to hold in the sense of wearing, then he is not God's and not Christ's through saving grace. To be in the Spirit, or to be sanctified and led by the Spirit, is to have the Spirit of God dwelling in the Christian. That sanctification is so joined and knit to the Christian's grafting into Christ, that it cannot be separated by any means. Anyone who does not have the Spirit in this way is not of Christ; they are not saved and do not have the Spirit.

This Spirit leading in believers is seen in three ways: being born again, spiritual-mindedness, and walking after the Spirit (Romans 8:4, 6, 9).

[1] The Spirit applies the work of Christ's redemption to the individual in what is called regeneration, or being born again from above by the Spirit (John 3:3, 5). This is the effectual operation of the Spirit on certain individuals to receive the benefits of Christ's death applied to them; only the Spirit can do this. This application of Christ's work is done by the Spirit's divine work on the human soul; on their heart. He blows like the wind, Jesus says, and gives spiritual birth to dead corpses wherever he wants, all over the earth from every tribe tongue and nation through the word. How happy are souls that have the Spirit blowing the wind of God's grace on them! Since Adam forfeited the Spirit in the garden, it is now part of the history of redemption to gain back the Spirit by God's gracious work through Christ and through the Spirit's work applying free grace to the heart. Men do not have the Spirit when they begin as fallen humans in Adam (Jude 19), and as a necessary consequence of that emptiness, they are sensual and carnal (1 Cor. 2:14). This

withdrawal of the Spirit in the garden is called "spiritual death." "But the natural man does not receive the things of the Spirit of God, for they are foolishness to him; nor can he know them, because they are spiritually discerned," (1 Cor. 2:14). He cannot know them because he is spiritually dead, until the Spirit blows on him.

Now, people must be regenerated and endowed with the Spirit of God, without which they have no spiritual eyes. Unless one is born from above, he cannot understand anything of the Spirit, Christ says in John 3. Christ demonstrates, emphatically, that men must be born again, or born from above, which is the work of regeneration on the heart of the wicked, or they have no hope of heaven. As John 6:63 states, "It is the Spirit who gives life; the flesh profits nothing." What does it profit? Some? A little? Such a sovereign spiritual birth (a change of the heart from stone to beating flesh) is by the blowing will of the Spirit (John 3:1-8). The Spirit convicts and sanctifies the individual by purging unbelief (John 16:8). It is so radical a change that those born again are then called new creatures (2 Cor. 5:17). Then, the Spirit inhabits the whole man and renews the whole man (Romans 8:9) with a vital principle of life in them. These are adopted as sons and daughters, and are assured by the Spirit of his sovereign choice of them for spiritual life (Rom. 8:16; 1 John 3:2). All of this is applied to them because of what the Anointed Savior did in satisfying God's just requirement in the law, and crediting them with his own righteousness and salvation. His work credited to their account. There is nothing they can do or could do.

[2] The Spirit then enables born again Christians to discern good from evil, or better yet, sin from holiness. He disposes the mind to accept a rational biblical truth and to know what the Scriptures contain. False teachers will always say, Christianity is irrational because one just believes because they are supposed to believe. That is an irrational statement, about the Christian religion, for Christianity is eminently rational; to be thought about, and believed based on evidence in the word as the word of God. Here the Spirit enlightens the Christian in expounding Scripture in order to apply that Scripture to the Christian's life and cause them to further grow in the mystical union he now has with Christ (1 Cor. 6:17). The Spirit illuminates through his indwelling presence within the individual (John 16:16; 2 Tim. 1:14; Rom. 8:9; Gal. 4:6; 1 Cor. 3:16; 1 John 4:13; Eph. 1:13). Those who are illuminated and are indwelt by the Spirit are led by the Spirit (Gal 5:18; Rom. 8:14; Ezek. 36:27). Indwelling then grants illumination to the bible, and this is what Paul is arguing for in Romans 8 – that is being led. People often think that all this talk about the Spirit is all done by some kind of zapping, without work, without study, without reading and such. This is the position of the charismatics of the last 150 years. They think the Spirit in them is a feeling. They think there are some with the Spirit who perform certain super-gifts, and others who don't have as much of the Spirit who do not. This is

garbage. The leading of the Spirit is given to all those born again – they are baptized, indwelt, empowered for service, and all the benefits of Christ are given to them. There is not a regular gas Christian and another who has high octane.

All those of Christ's body are baptized in the Spirit, and are led by the Spirit. Even the security of believers for the perseverance of the saints is the leading of the Spirit. And yet, this leading of the Spirit is always done through the word, in connection to it. These new Spirit-led virtuous actions of the Christian come after being born again, never before, and reside only in connection with the indwelling of the Spirit motioning them to good works: where shall they find these good works? Christian principles, in every way, are an immediate result of the Spirit's work on the believer through the word. Good works, then, are the fruit of the Spirit through the word. They are never isolated from Christ or the relations of his kingdom and are communicated to Christians by the Spirit through the Living Word. Love is the principle here, and only through the power of the Spirit can there be true Christian love reflecting Christ (1 Cor. 13). Love to Christ, love to the Word of Christ produces fruit. And the degree of a Christian's holy work will differ according to the Spirit's will. Romans 7 gives Christians a glimpse into the real struggle in which every believer fights against sin. They sometimes lose and sometimes win; they might even think they mostly lose, but in

Christ they always win. Ultimately, they will be glorified. But the Spirit of grace enables them to fight their way out of every temptation (1 Cor. 10:13), although believers do not always arrest that opportunity to please God and rather, they grieve the Spirit many times. As Ephesians 4:30 says, "And do not grieve the Holy Spirit of God, by whom you were sealed for the day of redemption."

[3] Yet, only through walking after the Spirit, with Christ, can Christians please God. Only through the Spirit is there any reformation of life. There is no virtuous act in the sight of God that Christians may entertain, much less do, than in conjunction with the sin-destroying power of the Spirit, and the holiness-enabling power of the Spirit. The Spirit ministers free grace to the Christian. Only through this free grace are they able to rest in Christ, and work works of righteousness before him. Only in the Spirit are they able to please God. This pleasing God, this reformation of life in walking in the Spirit, is accomplished by two parts that are inseparably joined together; the secret to a victorious walking with God is this: the Spirit leading through the Word.[8] The Christian cannot function in one without the other. This gives a great rebuke to those charismatic Christians that function, or try to function, *only in the Spirit* without the Word of God. It is impossible to do that.

---

[8] See my work on "Abundant Life" published by Puritan Publications, for a full study of this.

Many believe that having the Spirit, somehow the Spirit zaps them into some holiness, or zaps them into some knowledge. This zapping theory demonstrates that such people are confused with what the enlightening power of the Spirit means. Such a view is given by those not taught by the Spirit, not led by the Spirit, contrary to the Scriptures. Through the Word the Christian walks in the Spirit and the Spirit sanctifies the believer. This is why the doctrine of reformation is impossible without the Spirit. The Christian is engaged in doing something, some duty, they know from the Bible that it will in turn help them either kill sin, or enliven graces in them to be more zealous to God. Killing sin is called *mortification*. Enlivening grace is called *vivification*. The Spirit of God is engaged in both, but they are done through the instruction of the Word. Thomas Brooks said, "Every child of God has a twofold guide: the word without, and the Spirit within."[9] It is never by an unconscious assimilation of ideas that such killing of sin takes place in conformity to Jesus Christ. Christians don't sleep away sin while the Spirit works on them while they are dreaming or resting. It is always by holy duties, empowered spiritually by the Spirit of Grace on the mind through the word. This is why fleshly people cannot please God. It is why they have no power to do it.

This kind of sin-destroying power, this kind of life-enabling power, this kind of conformity to Jesus is

---

[9] The Complete Works of Thomas Brooks (Vol. 2).

by the Spirit's power *alone*. Jesus himself said, "Behold, I send the Promise of My Father upon you; but tarry in the city of Jerusalem until you are endued with power from on high," (Luke 24:49). They couldn't even share the Gospel rightly without being empowered by the Spirit. Does the Bible prove out this Spirit and Word connection in this way? "The Spirit of the LORD spoke by me, And His word was on my tongue," (2 Sam. 23:2). "This is the word of the LORD to Zerubbabel: `Not by might nor by power, but by My Spirit,' Says the LORD of hosts," (Zech. 4:6). "And when they had prayed, the place where they were assembled together was shaken; and they were all filled with the Holy Spirit, and they spoke the word of God with boldness," (Acts 4:31). "While Peter was still speaking these words, the Holy Spirit fell upon all those who heard the word," (Acts 10:44). "And take the helmet of salvation, and the sword of the Spirit, which is the word of God," (Eph. 6:17). "For our gospel did not come to you in word only, but also in power, and in the Holy Spirit," (1 Thess. 1:5). "Having received the word in much affliction, with joy of the Holy Spirit," (1 Thess. 1:6).

Not having the *Spirit* means no reformation of life. People who do not have the Spirit, do not have Jesus. "Now if anyone does not have the Spirit of Christ, he is not His," (Rom. 8:9). Jesus has ownership of all things. He is the sovereign Lord of all creation. He judges the nations. He holds the power of God and wields it in justice and judgment. He owns lost men. He owns saved men. His providential work as God the Son extends to all. But this passage is not speaking about God's sovereign right of ownership to creation. It is speaking about the indwelling power of the Spirit to his mystical body; to redeemed people. Those in the Spirit, and even those who will someday be in the Spirit, and all those who have ever been in the Spirit, are Christ's special ownership, the apple of his eye, the bride adorned for her husband. They have a special gift, an indwelling principle of spiritual power that others do not have. Such covenant ownership is due to Christ for all he accomplished on behalf of his people and his church as the sole Redeemer of men. And the seal of this covenant, the receipt to the blood bought purchase, is the indwelling Spirit of Christ. This is why the contrast is made by Paul about two kinds of people. Those who are led by the hand of the Spirit engage in reformation of life every day to Christ's glory. They are led to the Word, to be washed, and cleansed and made whole by Christ. Christ, the Word.

In contrast, those who are in the flesh cannot please God, then what are the consequences of attempting reformation of life on their own without the Spirit of Christ? To attempt reformation of life in the flesh through the Word is impossible. "Be holy as God is holy." How will one do this without the Spirit of holiness? "Walk in the Spirit." How will one do this without the "Spirit of Faith"? "Turn from these useless things to the living God," (Acts 14:15). How can they turn without the Spirit of Grace? "Repent, and believe in the gospel," (Mark 1:15). How will they do this without the "Spirit of Life"? "Believe on the name of His Son Jesus Christ," (1 John 3:23). How can one do this without the, "Spirit of Truth?" "Those who are in the flesh cannot please God," (Rom. 8:8). They have no power to please him. One is either lead by the Spirit, or left to themselves, dead in their sin.

What does *your* Spirit led walk look like? What does it look like to be led by the Spirit? We live for God through Christ by the Spirit. If we look for reformation of life, to be conformed into the image of Christ day by day, though I know we would like it to be much quicker than that, there are certain truths we simply have to hold steadfast to in order to be led by the Spirit through the Word to Jesus Christ. Only in Christ can our life please God (Eph. 1:6), that is, in him with whom the Father is well pleased (Matt. 3:17). There is no reformation of life without Christ. There is no reformation of life alone. It cannot be performed by you personally apart from the Spirit's free grace. We must be persuaded that Christ by his own merit acquired the Spirit for us (John 16:7). It is by the Spirit we are made alive (Rom. 8:2,11) and are led (Rom. 8:14). Otherwise we would be dead in sins, that is, unfit for every good work—in fact, predisposed to every evil work, God haters and Christ haters. Christ, united with us by faith, makes us, who were dead, alive in the Spirit (Eph. 2:4-7). He instills in us and communicates to us strength for living to God; as the root gives strength to the tree, and the head to the members of the body (John 15:4) so Christ gives us life in the Spirit. He is the one, by the Spirit, who brings forth the strength communicated to us; he motions it toward an action, and makes it fruitful in us (John 15:5), without which we can do nothing. Christ prescribes to us the laws for living to God (Matt. 5:2), and not only that, but incarnate, he goes before us by his very example being led by the Spirit in all things (Matt. 11:29; Phil. 2:5). And if all that were not enough, Jesus Christ himself lives in us (Gal. 2:20). He takes up residence in us so that all our abilities in such a way, in all things, at all times, and everywhere, Christ's humility, Christ's obedience, Christ's holiness, and Christ's imputed righteousness shines in us; this is what God loves to see when he looks at us – Christ shining back. Christ is our life. Christ's very life is made manifest in us (2 Cor. 4:11) by the leading of the Spirit.

The Spirit of Christ is not only a Spirit of manifestation and of revelation, but it is also a Spirit of supplication and of leading. It leads us by the hand to the Father. "As many as are led by the Spirit of God, they are the Sons of God," (Rom. 8:14). We have nothing to do with Christ, unless we are led by his Spirit in the word. In opposition to this, those separated from this special union with Christ, not having the Spirit in them (Rom. 8:9, 14), it shows that Christ does not live in them (Gal. 2:20).

How do you see your reformation of life in your good works? For you to reform in your life, is to leave off that which is sin, and take up those things that God has commanded to be done in his word. This is not legalism, rather, it is obedience to the Lord. The excuse of legalism in holy duties is a fruit of not being led by the Spirit, and making excuses so that one does not have to conform to Christ's image. Reformation of life in this way for you is only set down by God, and comes from his word, which the Spirit shines an enlightening light upon you as you read it and study it for the good of your soul. Micah 6:8, "He hath shewed thee, O man, what is good; and what doth the LORD require of thee, but to do justly, and to love mercy, and to walk humbly with thy God?" Where has he shown this? Rom. 12:2; Heb. 13:21! All the good works that the Spirit of God leads you in, are the fruits and evidence of a true and lively faith found in the word. "Seest thou how faith wrought with his works, and by works was faith made perfect?" (James 2:22). For you, assurance of salvation is greatly strengthened as you see your life being more and more led into the good works of the Spirit's leading. In such works, you glorify God, because you are his workmanship created in Christ Jesus for good works. And in these works, in all the Reformation of life that you press into, the Spirit makes such works fruits to holiness; the Spirit does that, you don't. These fruits ultimately point you to the end of all this, which is Christ's precious gift of eternal life to you.

This is that which he works in you by free grace. "But now being made free from sin, and become servants to God, ye have your fruit unto holiness, and the end everlasting life." (Rom. 6:22).

Your ability to this end is not at all from yourself. All of this is wholly from the Spirit of Christ, from grace, for tender mercies showered on you. You are simply enabled by the Spirit to do them, (Ezek. 36:26-27; John 15:4-6). There is in you, in that indwelling principle of life, the actual influence of the Holy Spirit working his good pleasure in you; day by day, (Phil 2:13; 4:13; 2 Cor 3:5).

Consider three points of assurance in being led by the Spirit. Three things the Spirit does in assuring you of true reformation of life by his indwelling.

[1] This reform is always, and in every way, founded on the divine truth of the promises of salvation illuminated by the Spirit. "Wherein God, willing more abundantly to shew unto the heirs of promise the immutability of his counsel, confirmed it by an oath:" (Heb. 6:17). The immutability of God and his word is the first. The promises held in it are true and just and right, and they paint the picture of the fallen condition which the first Adam plummeted humankind into, and the redemption that the second Adam accomplished to save believing sinners, granting them eternal life. It is all through the word that Christ's free grace is found. Promises, promises, promises to you *personally* sent by Christ through the illumination of the Spirit in the

word; that is the first assurance – the promises of God believed as true and good by you.

[2] Good works that you do in the Spirit. This reform is always, and at all times, believed inwardly in your heart, and you have a certainty which is not of yourselves of the evidence of those graces to which these promises are made and you outwardly exemplify those truths in your life. "Whereby are given unto us exceeding great and precious promises: that by these ye [that's you] might be partakers of the divine nature, having escaped the corruption that is in the world through lust," (2 Peter 1:4). "And hereby we do know that we know him, if we keep his commandments," (1 John 2:3). "For our rejoicing is this, the testimony of our conscience, that in simplicity and godly sincerity, not with fleshly wisdom, but by the grace of God, we have had our conversation in the world, and more abundantly to you-ward," (2 Cor. 1:12). Your good works testify of your sonship. Not perfect works, but good works. Christ perfected the work, and you shadow that work. And God accepts that work as if Christ has done it, because he has. So, the promises, and good works testify. And a third?

[3] And then, you have the testimony of the Spirit of adoption witnessing with your spirit that you are a child of God. Assurance of being led by the Spirit of God, is more than simply collecting quotes out of the bible. One of the greatest assurances comes from the internal witness of the Holy Spirit which testifies to us

through the Word of God that we are sons and daughters of God. Romans 8:16 says, "The Spirit himself bears witness with our spirit that we are children of God." That's true, you think to yourself as you read, but you add to it, and it is true of me because of the grace I have received in Christ. This gives way to the sealing of the Holy Spirit as Paul writes in Ephesians 1:13, "In him you also, when you heard the word of truth, the Gospel of your salvation, and believed in him, were sealed with the promised Holy Spirit." When you read the Scripture and believe the promise, the Spirit seals that in your heart. The Spirit testifying of the truth of the application of those Scriptures you read. The Spirit is "a Spirit of truth" who is a "teacher" leading us into all truth. He makes us "God-taught," (διδακτοὶ θεοῦ John 6:45; 14:17; 16:13). He gives us as "a witness" an infallible testimony of the grace of God and of Christ (John 15:26; 16:14) concerning our state when "he witnesses with our spirit that we are the sons of God" (Rom. 8:16). He produces in us a certainty. Chrysostom said, "What doubt is left here? If a man, or an angel should make a promise, perhaps some might doubt, but if the supreme Essence, the Spirit of God, who causes us to pray, makes a promise to those praying, bestows the promise, giving the testimony to us within, what room is there for doubt?"[10] He is in fact, the Spirit of Consolation, of comfort, where the believer is to rest on him and his leading them to Christ's promises. "Surely goodness and

---

[10] "Homily 14," On Romans [NPNF1, 11:442; PG 60.527J].

mercy shall follow me all the days of my life," (Psa. 23:6). Rom. 8:38 says, "I am persuaded that nothing shall be able to separate us from the love of God in Christ." What a great persuasion! Nothing can separate you from the love of God, from the work of Christ, from the leading of the Spirit. So, you have the promise of the word, the good works of your Spirit led walk, and the internal testimony of the Spirit in your heart that you are assured of free grace in Christ. There is in this much reliance on the Spirit of Christ for our good in this.

So then, as Paul explains, what can be done at any stage of the Christian life without the Spirit of Christ? Nothing. What good can come by us? Nothing. What work can we work before Christ that is pleasing? Nothing. What hope can we conjure up? Nothing. What further change can we fabricate in our souls? Nothing. What can replace the work of the Spirit in us? Nothing. What can we do before Christ without his Spirit for our good? Nothing. Why? Reformation of life is *impossible* without the Spirit of God.

Appendix

I WANT TO BE REFORMED!

Do you want to be reformed? The idea of *reformation* is simply a nickname for *zealous and unwavering biblical sanctification;* a sanctification that continues in Christ after Christ has begun the work in you. "For this is the will of God, even your sanctification," (1 Thess. 4:3). "And if ye will not be reformed by me by these things, but will walk contrary unto me; Then will I also walk contrary unto you, and will punish you yet seven times for your sins," (Lev. 26:23-24). The term reformation should be a word that you use as a starting point. I ask you again, *do you want to be reformed?* If you do, then you want to be sanctified by the Holy Spirit to be conformed into the blessed image of our Lord and Savior Jesus Christ. To be more like Jesus Christ is to continually be reforming, to continually be *sanctified.* "For whom he did foreknow, he also did predestinate to be conformed to the image of his Son," (Rom. 8:29).[1] This directly relates to the means and manner that the church takes to press on toward a full orbed reformation both in the heart and in the mind. The church should be pressing into the Kingdom, pressing onward to see revival continually cultivated in our life (individually), family (as a little church), church

---

[1] See also Romans 12:2.

(in our worship and work) and nation (in our progression to dominate the world and arrest it by the work of the Gospel of Christ).

Do you *expect* reformation? In many ways reformation has *already* occurred. You are living *in it*. You are even experiencing it as you turn page after page of biblical material, like this work on exhorting you to a full reformation. You can go on the internet and find resources that cater to biblical reformation. You can walk into any Walmart and pick up a copy of the Bible for $5. Reformation for king Josiah was *finding* the book of the law and then to do what the book of the Law said. Reformation, for the magisterial reformers like Luther and Calvin, was to *rescue* the Bible, in many respects, from the Roman Catholic Church which subverted the Gospel from the people and hid it. They too were finding the book of the Law again. But today we *have* the Bible, and we *have* reformed resources. What then, for us today, does *reformation* mean?

Let me ask you, did you go into your church service this past Lord's Day thinking, "Today, we will have *real* revival." If you are a minister, did you look at your sermon notes reflecting on the reality that God could, at that moment, use *your sermon* to invoke a revival of the highest magnitude in your congregation, and that you would be the means for the next great awakening? It was said of Charles Spurgeon that every time he walked up into his pulpit to preach he would say to himself at each step, "I believe in the Holy Spirit." He relied on the Spirit and so prayed as he entered the pulpit to preach for the Spirit's work to be accomplished. No doubt, when Jonathan Edwards preached his famous sermon "Sinners in the Hands of an Angry God," twice in one Sunday, that he was not "expecting," so to speak, revival on the second delivery of that message. He chose, "A Narrative of *Surprising* Conversions" as the title of his work in explaining what was happening when the Spirit of God began *the Great Awakening.* He was "surprised" at such a thing. Does that mean Edwards or Spurgeon or other countless examples like this mean that they did not believe in reformation? Or did they have a different idea about reformation? Instances like these do not negate the excitement and hope of seeing true reformation occur in our day, *whatever that might mean.* The Reformers, the Westminster Divines, Edwards and Spurgeon all lived in times where the word of God, the church, the work of the Spirit, *etc.,* did in fact exist, and in *great* measure. The reality that, such times demonstrated the acquisition of the Word of God and the weekly preaching of the word of God *assumes* revival and reformation in those very means of grace! Why then do we not see more revivals breaking out across the land?

It matters both how reformation in religion begins, and *continues,* lest it ends by God's furious hand in his wrath and displeasure. Knowing that God is the catalyst of continued reformation, (*i.e.* that God makes revival happen by the power of his Spirit through the word of God for the glory of Christ), at the same time, he can make it end as abruptly as it begins because of man's inability to continue the work.[2] Do you want the revival of religion in your own church? Would you like to see hearty reformation, or maybe we might say, *continued* reformation? What Christian would not?

Since, truly, *reformation has already begun*, we ought not to lose heart, and steadily keep it *moving*. This presents a myriad of problems for professing Christians since, 1) we are tainted with sin,[3] 2) we get lazy,[4] 3) we get forgetful,[5] 4) we get cooled in our zeal,[6] 5) we compromise,[7] and 6) we live in a country (wherever that might be) that is sin-ridden and overwhelmingly hates God.[8] Will God continue to bless us in such cases? Does

---

[2] And for those of you who are familiar with the militant overtaking of the Lord Protector just at the time the 1647 Westminster Confession was completed, one can see the historical significance of a delayed or stopped reform.

[3] Hebrews 12:1; Matt. 10:37-38; Luke 8:14, 9:59-62, 12:15, 14:26-33, 18:22-25, 21:34; Romans 7:1ff, 13:11-14; 2 Cor. 7:1; Eph. 4:22-24; Col. 3:5-8; 1 Tim. 6:9-10; 2 Tim. 2:4; 1 Peter 2:1, 4:2; 1 John 2:15-16.

[4] Prov. 6:6, 9–11, 24:33, 10:4-5, 26, 12:9, 24, 27, 13:4, 14:23, 15:19, 18:9, 19:15, 24, 20:4, 13, 21:25-26, 23:21, 24:30-31, 33,34, 26:13, 26:14–16; Eccl. 4:5, 10:18; Isa. 56:10; Ezek. 16:49; Luke 19:20–25; Matt. 20:6-7, 25:26-27; Acts 17:21; Rom. 12:11; 2 Thess. 3:10-11; 1 Tim. 5:13; Heb. 6:12.

[5] Forgetting God is forgetting his covenant, Deut. 4:23; 2 Kings 17:38; His works, Psa. 78:7, 11, 106:13; His benefits, Psa. 103:2; 106:7; His word, Heb. 12:5; Jas. 1:25; His Law, Psa. 119:153, 176; Hos. 4:6; His church, Psa. 137:5; His past deliverances, Judg. 8:34; Psa. 78:42; His power to deliver, Isa. 51:13-15.

[6] Matthew 24:12; Rev. 3:15-16.

[7] Scripture calls this being double minded. James 1:8, 4:8.

[8] The wicked forget God, which is a characteristic, Prov. 2:17; Isa. 65:11. Backsliders guilty of forgetting God, Jer. 2:32, 3:21.

God have a *toleration* point? God's wrath will one day be poured forth on the wicked (wicked people *and* wicked nations) from the cup of his indignation. 1 Thessalonians 2:16 describes those who, "always live to fill up the measure of their sins until wrath comes upon them to the uttermost." Genesis 15:16 directs us that God has set a specific time to judge the wicked Amorites, to judge *nations*, "The iniquity of the Amorites is not yet full." Every day men fill up their sins, but there is a specific measuring point which God allows, which only God knows. We ought never to squander away, in whatever fashion, true reformation and revival.

You, reader, are obliged to be reformed by God's directives in the Word. Is God pleased with the nation in which you live? Is he pleased with your community? Your church? Your own life? Is there a need to *rekindle* your zeal for true biblical reformation which you already possess in this information laden age? Christians must not believe that it is too late to *revive* reformation. It is not too late, nor ever too late, to believe that God can save reformation from becoming desolation,[9] and instead turn it into a revival of religion. Reformation must be extensive, zealous, and long term. Such a reform will only take place by God's method, and power.[10]

---

[9] See Stephen Marshall's excellent work, "Reformation or Desolation" published by Puritan Publications.

[10] Revivals occurred biblically under *Joshua*, Josh. 5:2–9; *Samuel*, 1 Sam. 7:1–6; *Elijah*, 1 Kings 18:17–40; *Jehoash and Jehoiada*, 2 Kings 11: 12; 2 Chr. 23:24; *Hezekiah*, 2 Kings 18:1–7; 2 Chr. 29–31; *Josiah*, 2 Kings 22:23; 2 Chr. 34:35; *Asa*, 2 Chr. 14:2–5; 15:1–14; *Manasseh*, 2 Chr. 33:12–19. They are seen in foreign nations like *Nineveh*, Jonah

As Christians we must never forget that we have already experienced a reformation. What we need today is to continue the reformation already begun and pray that the word of God as found, plainly given to us in Scripture, and taught in documents like these from reformed times, will penetrate our hearts and mind that we might be on fire with a holy zeal for the glory of God.

3:4–10. At *Pentecost*, and *post-pentecostal times*, Acts 2:1–42, 46, 47; 4:4, 5:14; 6:7, 9:35, 11:20-21, 12:24, 14:1, 19:17–20.

Other Helpful Books
by Puritan Publications

5 Marks of a Biblical Church by C. Matthew McMahon

5 Marks of a Biblical Disciple by C. Matthew McMahon

5 Marks of a Biblical Commitment to the Visible Body of Christ by C. Matthew McMahon

The Wickedness, Humiliation, Restoration and Reformation of Manasseh by C. Matthew McMahon

The Duty of Reformation in Light of God's Mercies by Thomas Gouge (1605-1681)

Reformation and Desolation, by Stephen Marshall (1594–1655)

The Christian's Duty Towards Reformation by Thomas Ford (1598–1674)

The Precious Seeds of Reformation by Humphrey Hardwicke (n.d.)

Gradual Reformation Intolerable by C. Matthew McMahon and Anthony Burgess (1600-1663)

Church Reformation Tenderly Handled by John Brinsley (1600-1665)

Family Reformation Promoted, and Other Works by Daniel Cawdrey (1588-1664)

A Discourse on Church Discipline and Reformation by Daniel Cawdrey (1588-1664)